Mothers in
Transition

Mothers in Transition

A Study of the Changing Life Course

by

Pamela S. Eakins

SCHENKMAN PUBLISHING COMPANY, INC.
CAMBRIDGE, MASSACHUSETTS

Copyright © 1983

Schenkman Publishing Company, Inc.
3 Mount Auburn Place
Cambridge, MA 02138

Library of Congress Cataloging in Publication Data

Eakins, Pamela S.
  Mothers in transition

  Bibliography: p.
  1. Mothers – United States. 2. Mothers – Employment –
United States. I. Title.
HQ759.E17   306.8'7   81-13581
ISBN 0-87073-475-X   AACR2
ISBN 0-87073-476-8 (pbk.)

Printed in the United States of America

Acknowledgments

I would like to thank Blaine E. Mercer for constant support and critical editing of earlier drafts of this work. For invaluable comments and criticism on the formulation of the project, thanks go to Janice L. Demarest, E. Merle Adams and Robert M. Hunter.

Bernhard M. Haisch deserves special praise for suffering through each word at least ten times.

My greatest debt, however, is to the forty-five women who shared their lives with me. I will always feel a special bond with each one of them.

For
Mary Louise
Joyce
George
& Bernhard

Contents

List of Tables

List of Figures

Introduction
by Jessie Bernard

There was a time when the lives of women could be encompassed in three stages, the years before childbearing, the years of childbearing, and the years after childbearing (Bernard, 1980). These stages were of fairly sizeable duration and of fairly uniform specifications. As in the case of males — on whose lives most discussions of life cycles have been based until recently (Chickering, 1981) — when civilizations became more complex, so also did the lives of females. The number of stages grew (Bernard, 1975). We have had to insert new ones from time to time. The stage of infancy comes to be divided into "premies," neonates, and more developed newborns at the other end of the age spectrum we find we have to distinguish the young-old from the old-old. We now recognize early, middle, and late childhood. The stage of adolescence had to be inserted at the turn of the century and of youth, during the Depression several decades later. I do not doubt we will continue to have to subdivide the chronology of human existence as life in our complex society continues to differentiate our experience by age.

As stages have become proliferated, each one has come to cover a shorter period of time. Stage succeeds stage so rapidly that the very idea of stages has been superceded by the concept of transitions if not crises. We speak of the life course rather than of the life cycle. The term "course" conveys the dynamics of an onrushing stream of life. Almost before we can turn around the infant has become a toddler; almost before we are ready to recognize it, the young-old have become the old-old. And so on.

It is fitting, therefore, that this book should emphasize transitions in the life course of mothers. The forty-five mothers we meet here, 27–60 years of age in the late '70s and early '80s when they were studied, have already been through a large number of transitions by the time we meet them. The first, from school into marriage (pp. 7–30), includes the processes which have propelled young women into marriage. The second transition was into becoming a housewife (pp. 30–39); the third, into an expanding family circle as children were born (pp. 39–43), 57–76); the fourth, into the peak stage of motherhood and the full-house plateau (pp. 43–48); the fifth, into the shrinking circle stage (pp. 48–54) – the stage the women are in when we meet them, a stage characterized by an "identity-integrity" crisis which they are meeting by return to college. The sixth stage, the minimal circle stage (pp. 54–55) is not explored here. It is one the women studied here are hoping to postpone or circumvent. They are preparing by "reengagement" to take up the time slack which reduced family obligations generate.

In the earlier transitions – into marriage and the several stages of motherhood – the women were following well-charted paths. They had been programmed for the specifications of the roles they were entering. The transitions may have been difficult but there were models, the course was familiar, support was available. Willy-nilly, ready or not, they had passed from one to the other. All the norms of the female world embodied in customs, traditions, mores, collective attitudes, beliefs, and legal norms acted like "cilia" to propel them into marriage and into motherhood. They had adapted, accommodated, even sacrificed for their families according to the love and/or duty ethos of the female world (Bernard, 1981). And as long as they performed according to the script, regardless of how they felt about it, they were taken for granted. No kudos were forthcoming. Of course they put their families first.

But the relatively recent transition this book zeroes in on – from full-time housewife-and-mother to part-time housewife-and-student – usually in the shrinking circle stage, is vastly different. Transition to re-entry into college, or "reengagement," is for many women counter-cultural, an individual choice, not prescribed. In some circles their view of children as "transitory" (120) may even be "deviant" in a pejorative sense. In this book we watch them struggle with the problems involved and root for them.

The entrance of mothers into the labor force has been called a "subtle revolution" (Smith, 1979). The women we meet here are preparing for careers and we can see how subtle this revolution has been. The women themselves are only dimly aware of its ramifications. They see it as personal, individual until they are well involved in it. This is a transition they have not been programmed for. No one could say that they had been coerced into it by social pressures. There was no great pressure on them to enter the labor force; if anything, there was resistance to it on the part of friends, even family. It may have been a necessary transition for financial reasons, but not always so. Nor was it always without cost to the marriage. Husbands were sometimes negative, even resentful (p. 98). Some children were supportive, but others were variable or indifferent in their attitudes. Some objected when they did not have the accustomed maternal attention. All members felt they had a vested interest in the family status quo. Any change in the "even tenor of their ways" was disturbing.

Still, the psychological rewards for participating in this unscripted transition from full-time homemaker to student were spectacular (chapter 7). The women learned who they were; they found "labels" — I do not like the term — which defined them in legitimate roles as students, scholars, intellectuals, thinkers, doers. They found other women to share their newfound self-images. They did well in their courses. Quotations from the interviews reflect the exhileration of a great high (pp. 121–122, 124). Independence, power, personal satisfaction, stimulation, and validation echo and re-echo through them. They resemble the responses of women Joseph Katz told us about in an earlier study (1976): wonderfully braced, cheerful, optimistic. True, some had become divorced, but for many, marriage was better — for them if not for their husbands — than it had been before. The pluses mount up.

But the author does not allow us even this brief respite. She is not satisfied. She has been sheathing her sword. After her careful, conscientious presentation of research findings, in the end she unsheathes it. These women were the Horatia Algers of the reentry population. But many women are missing from their ranks. In the case of the absentees from this study, the love and/or duty ethos of the female world prevailed in decision-making when husbands, family, or friends objected. They are among the women who "drop out when the familial pressures become too great even though it may be crucial to their mental and physical health to continue to pursue their activities" (111). Many are doubtless among those who show up in epidemiological studies of the depressed population (Bernard, 1972).

The author's critique of marriage — the starting point of the transition from housewife to student — , of the transition program itself, and of the probable outcome is devastating. She spares neither marriage, reentering programs, nor the status quo.

For the last decade researchers have been trying to pinpoint the aspects of marriage which are so dysfunctional for women (Bernard, 1972). This book clarifies some of them. Here are women who – in conformity to the ethos of the female world (Bernard)–have adapted, accommodated, served, sacrificed, put others first. They have invested in husbands' careers and adapted to the exigencies of such male careers, often at the expense of their own development. Now, in the stage of shrinking family obligations, they suffer from feelings of entrapment, imprisonment, boredom, powerlessness, cabin fever; from feelings of resentment at being left behind as husbands forge ahead in their careers; from longing for self-fulfillment, achievement.

Now an opportunity has become available to them to do what they have wanted to do – always, to be sure, making time to take care of their families, even at their own expense – and they have taken advantage of it. They return to school and thus, hopefully, to careers. But, Eakins tells us, they have, in effect, been betrayed.

She is no more sparing of reentry programs than of marriage. They are too accommodative, too remedial, too separatist. They accept too complacently the discontinuities built into mothers' lives. Nor do they adequately prepare the women for the world outside, for the discrimination they will encounter in the labor force. Nor do they prepare women for nontraditional professions. Although the women become more feminist in orientation, most of them prepare for the age-old roles of women, the helping roles, as counselors, as personnel or social workers. They are, at best, prepared only for more service, more helping. Paid, to be sure, but still in the old female mold. The problems are perpetuated, not remedied.

Meanwhile, at the other end of the transition, the world of work, the old status quo persists. Sexism and ageism are still there. The years out for marriage and motherhood have greatly disadvantaged the women for serious professional advancement in a world that plays hard ball, a world that does not permit such discontinuities. Eakins does not explicitly say "what fools these [female] mortals be." She is too compassionate to blame the victim. But that is a possible conclusion one might arrive at.

I understand the author's conclusions from her research. I am not as despairing as she seems to be. I can understand why she wants so much more for these women, why she finds both the preparation for the outside world offered by the schools and the economy they are being prepared to enter so far from meeting the challenges of this day and age. I share with her the wish that the schools were able to do more; I, too, would like to see a less status-quo accommodation. I, too, hope for the day when sexism and ageism will disappear from the scene. To justify my own patience I often have occasion to remind my young feminist consoeurs that one has to have lived a long time—as I have—in order to be hopeful, if not necessarily optimistic, about the future for women. Any social movement needs not only anger but also hope, or one ends in futility. The author's portrait of the mothers—her Horatia Algers—in this book is reassuring to me. To them I can only say, God speed! At least some of them will beat the odds. Some may even change them. To all, the accolades due anyone willing to participate in this revolution. And kudos to Ms. Eakins herself who has invested so much effort on their behalf and shown so much concern for their success.

1
The "Reengaging" Mother

In recent years the structure of the lives of mothers has changed significantly. The childbearing years are concentrated into a shorter period than ever before. Further, the financial stability of the family has become precarious.

As a result, women are entering the paid labor force in ever greater numbers. We are now witnessing subtle and overt alterations of the "social fabric" of American society.

And although some of these changes have been desired by mothers, many have not. Most often women are finding themselves caught in the tides of social change, struggling to leave old norms behind while striving to accept new ones. Whether they are content with the changes, indifferent, or angry, individual women are discovering that these changes have caused them to personally reevaluate their priorities and set new goals.

Out of economic need, women must often go to work in the marketplace. Yet most women have not been socialized to expect to incur this activity as an adult role. Further, they may be forced to work exactly at that point in life when they had expected to "retire" from their major adult work roles as the bearers and socializers of children. Ambivalence toward society and themselves as individuals may be the result,

1

ambivalence concerning their roles, expectations, and status in the social realm.

Many women have found themselves caught between a rock and a hard place. They had expected to marry. They had expected to bear children. They had expected to care for husbands and households, and to cultivate their greatest gift, inspiring and nurturing the gifts of others.

All of this — at the price of neglecting their own talents. And suddenly, society seemed to have turned the tables! Women must go to work, but they are unprepared. Their knowledge is obsolete, or the clerical jobs, which they have moved in and out of as a result of family need, no longer seem lucrative or meaningful as a permanent, full-time involvement.

Trying to stay afloat in the ripples of this uncertain situation is not easy. In droves, women are seeking retraining to enter or renter the job market. Often this training comes via local colleges and universities. The number of reentering women has been consistently on the rise over the past two decades and this phenomenon crosses all generations of women.

It is these "reengaging" women with whom this study is concerned.

The "Disengaged" Mother

Going to work after an absence from the paid labor force has become routine for women and college becomes a logical step in achieving this objective.

This phenomenon has come to be known as "reentry" or "reengagement" and these terms are widely used in conjunction with college programs which seek to involve housewives over twenty-five years of age in the college curriculum.

To reengage implies that one has been disengaged. Sociology has an area of study called "disengagement theory," which refers primarily to a process elderly people go through before dying. It may be useful to compare "disengagement" as used in this sense with the "disengagement" women experience upon becoming wives and mothers.

Disengagement has referred to ". . . an inevitable process in which the individual reduces the number of his interpersonal relationships and alters the quality of those that remain." (Cf. Atchley, 1972) Individual disengagement is seen as selective. In other words, the individual withdraws from some roles, but not from others. It is stated that the individual becomes increasingly preoccupied with him- or herself and it is held that the reduced frequency of interaction weakens the hold that norms have over the individual. In this way, the disengaged individual becomes liberated, freed from the constraint of norms.

On the other hand, when women marry and become housewives and mothers, they may, indeed, be disengaging from the norms which govern masculine behavior, yet they are *actively engaging* in the norms which govern women's lives. When women become housewives, they institutionalize the social mandate to marry. When they have babies, they are acting very much in accordance with social norms. Thus, for women, disengagement is a misnomer. Though it may imply reducing the number of social contacts, it also implies meeting a different but specific set of social expectations by entering into a traditional role complex.

Inherent in the terminology used to advertise and describe "reengagement programs" in colleges and universities is the assumption that clients have been disengaged. It is important to note that disengagement, in this sense, refers only to *disengagement from the work force.* Since participation in the work force is considered to be *representative of the ability to play an active role in influencing the technical development of society,* women who are not working are viewed as disengaged individuals, *disengaged from an active role in society.* This is particularly inappropriate in that, at this time, women may be *more actively involved in fulfilling their traditional roles in accordance with social expectations than at any other time in their lives.*

Reengagement programs may ironically serve to perpetuate women's current identity problems while attempting to integrate women "back into the mainstream." The disengagement/reengagement concept places specific value judgments on "women's work," traditional women's roles. It leaves women with the question: What are we supposed to do?

Nevertheless, these are the terms most commonly used. Thus, they will be employed throughout this treatise. We will, however, try to avoid the value-laden baggage they carry.

About the Study

Mothers in Transition seeks to examine the conditions under which reengaging women confront social change head-on in a personal sense. The study begins by looking at "woman's place" in recent years and how this has changed with regard to the educational and occupational spheres.

Next, *Mothers in Transition* explores the adult life cycle, concentrating on changes in women's traditional roles and the effect these have had on the nature of women's participation in society. The stages of life are elucidated in a phase by phase manner in order to shed more light on the status attainment process for women.

The nature of motherhood is then examined in some depth in terms of the decision-making power and the constraints that women associate with that role. We examine the mandate toward motherhood in this country and the contingencies involved in becoming a mother.

As women face periods of transition when children begin to leave home, they begin to reevaluate their situations and their identities, and search for alternative activities. Such turning points in women's lives are discussed with emphasis on social structure, perception of self, and the influence and attitudes of "significant others." The family, as a support system, is explored in conjunction with women's roles within the family. The type and amount of leeway, margins of freedom and variations for individual women are examined.

Mothers in Transition analyzes the changing individual woman, her drive to achieve and to overcome barriers, the extent of her success and her perceptions of power, marginality and the status of women in American society.

Various questions regarding behavior and motivation are posed. What causes these women to venture outside of their families into new situations or situations which they have not been in for years? Why do these women act the way they do in particular circumstances? Is it because of their own needs and expectations or in response to the needs and expectations of others? What factors influence women's performance and motivation? What can they expect to achieve and how do they feel about their achievements?

The phenomenon of reengagement among middle class women is increasing and is apparently the result of specific, deliberate points of decision which spring directly from the larger, overall framework of such women's adult life cycle structures. A comprehensive investigation of the adult life stages for these women is therefore necessary in order to understand the reengagement phenomenon, particularly with regard to structural changes in the housewife role in recent years.

Once we have a better grasp of women's adult life stages, we should be able to help individual women anticipate and prepare for reentry by appropriately structuring our educational and occupational systems. By attaining a better understanding of women's life stages and the conditions for achievement, we should understand, in a larger sense, the structural barriers to women's achievement. Such knowledge can provide the basis for restructuring society for the benefit of men and women in general.

Mothers in Transition is based on the experiences of forty-five reengaging women. The information they provided has been compiled through a process of interviewing, tape recording, and transcribing.

Herein lies the story of a group of women ranging in age from twenty-seven to sixty. They are women of various backgrounds, religions, educations and incomes. Most are of Caucasian origin and have enough money to live comfortably. All were in a state of flux when they volunteered to participate in the study.

Before we begin our expose of these women's lives, however, let us turn to look at the status attainment process for women, "woman's place" in current times.

2

The Traditional Woman and the Scheme of Things: Education, Marriage, and the Early Status Attainment Process

Beginning with High School

One of the most important preadult socializers is school and apparently high school girls are emerging from the formal school system socialized into ambivalence. They are ambivalent about what they want to do in their lives and, if they have something in mind, they are ambivalent as to how to attain it. This remains as true today as it was in the 1950s. How can this ambivalent attitude be explained?

In looking at two national samples of high school youth, first in 1955 and later in 1970, Karl Alexander and Bruce Eckland (1974) reached a number of conclusions. They discovered that females tend to outperform males in high school, yet they are less likely to be enrolled in any kind of college preparatory curriculum during their sophomore year. Also, girls expect lower levels of educational attainment and significant people in their lives have very little influence over their expectations. Alexander and Eckland found a strong correlation among males between ability and attainment, but among females the strongest correlation was between socioeconomic status and attainment. In other words, bright boys expected to continue with their education, but girls, regardless of intelli-

7

gence, generally expected to continue with their education only if they came from a family of high socioeconomic status. Thus, the males in the sample were more successful in converting their ability into educational payoffs. The effect of sex on expectations for educational attainment remained despite controls on academic ability, status background, performance, educational goal orientations, self-concept, curriculum enrollment and the influence of significant others. Alexander and Eckland were forced to conclude that school process variables do not account for female educational attainment.

Another study by Michael Hout and William Morgan (1975) compared the educational expectations and occupational expectations of high school students and found some similar results. For boys, educational expectations are mediated by parental encouragement and intelligence, which are equal determinants of grades. In addition, they found that grades determine parental encouragement, thus resulting in a reciprocal relationship between grades and parental encouragement. The influence of peers is also important in terms of projected expectations and actual performance for high school boys.

Discrepancies arise, however, when these variables are applied to high school girls. Hout and Morgan found that, for girls, intelligence alone determines grades and that good grades bring about parental encouragement but the inverse relationship does not hold. In addition, the father's occupation and the number of siblings have a direct effect on educational expectations, which concurs with Alexander's and Eckland's (1974) findings, but Hout and Morgan found that this relationship is mediated by parental encouragement. Peer relationships have only one third of the effect of parental expectations for girls.

With regard to occupational expectations, parental and peer expectations and degree of intelligence all have a major effect for boys, again, findings which concur with the status attainment literature, but for girls the relationships are not so clear cut. In fact, this model cannot specify at all the causes of occupational expectations in girls. Parental encouragement for educational expectations does not carry over to occupational expectations. Hout and Morgan conclude that perhaps girls do not make occupational plans at this time.

If the school process variables cannot explain educational expectations and the status attainment variables cannot explain occupational expectations for high school girls, what factors can account for these wide differentials in expectations for success? These studies suggest that different structural referents exist for each group. Hout and Morgan suggest that the inability of their model to explain occupational expectations for females may be due to the fact that stratification theory is generally addressed to the placement of white males in the social structure and the dominant variables do not account for female attainment.

Various researchers have noted that many assumptions underlie methods frequently used in status attainment studies. Among them are the following:

1. Stratification theory is based on the assumption of a "normal" family unit.
2. Differences of role, position and status within the family are not considered to be criteria of stratification.
3. Men and women within a family "unit" hold identical degrees of power, prestige and wealth. (Cf. Oakley, 1974)

As Ann Oakley (1974) states, these assumptions are false in that they imply that females have no resources of their own and that the family is a symmetrical status structure. Sociologists of the family recognize that the "normal" family unit is all but nonexistent (Cf. Skolnick, 1978). In addition, these assumptions do not take into account social and technical changes which are allowing for alterations in women's primary roles.

At the moment, it is unclear to investigators where women are headed with regard to their traditional roles and their "pioneer" roles in the labor market. Some state that an entirely new explanation of women's achievement is warranted. Others state that very little has actually changed for women with regard to their traditonal roles or their participation in the labor force. What is becoming very clear to sociologists, however, is that because of numerous assumptions we have made about women, women have been overlooked in a great number of sociological studies and it is time that we straighten out some of the myths that surround women's positions in society.

An Attempt to Make Sense of Attainment Differentials: Horner's "Motive to Avoid Success"

Matina Horner (1972) carried out studies of college students wherein she provided images of successful males and successful females and asked students to write stories about them. In the women's stories, she found the heroine berated, a result which did not hold true for the men's stories about the hero. She attributed these results to a "motive to avoid success" in females. This "fear of success," as it later came to be called, seemed to be particularly strong for high-achieving women. Horner provided the explanation that high achievers fear success because of the expectations or beliefs the individual has about the nature of the consequences of her actions. Fear of success depends on the value these consequences have to the individual. She stated that most women expect negative consequences to follow achievement in terms of social rejection and the stigma of being thought unfeminine. Horner claims that this "motive" extends to the intellectual, professional and personal lives of women in our society.

Essentially, Horner concluded that the most highly competent and otherwise achievement-motivated young women, when faced with a conflict between a feminine image and the expression of competence, adjust their behavior to internalized feminine sex role stereotypes. Thus, anticipating success might be regarded as an outright threat to women.

Matina Horner's ideas have gained a tremendous following and have been posited again and again in the literature on women's achievement as the major explanation of why the stratification or status attainment variables cannot account for women's success (or lack of it). However, researchers have tried to replicate her studies and have come up with dramatically different conclusions. In addition, some investigators have found problems with Horner's methods (Cf. Condry and Dyer, 1976: Levine and Crumrine, 1975). Why the mass appeal? The answer undoubtedly lies in the fact that the "motive to avoid success" begins to fill the gap in status attainment theory where women are concerned.

Eleanor Maccoby (1972) reached the conclusion that nontraditional girls, more career-oriented girls, would possess a higher intellectual ability than traditional girls. Edmund Doherty and Cathryn Culver (1976) in an exploration of sex role identification, ability and achievement in high school girls, tested Maccoby's conclusions together with Horner's conclusions that high IQ girls would be less likely to achieve because of the "motive to avoid success," and reported quite different results. They found that girls who perceived sex roles in a nontraditional sense scored higher on verbal intelligence. Yet, they also found that the more traditional the girls' values were, the higher was their class rank. Further, the more nontraditional the girls were, the more they envisioned completing college which does not support Horner's conclusions.

Doherty and Culver concluded that nontraditional girls of high school age probably have not fully utilized their intellectual ability. Their conclusions suggest that perhaps teachers are reinforcing sex roles by rewarding those girls with a more traditional outlook. They suggest that high ability, independent high school girls are probably not provided with the opportunities, options or encouragement which would allow them maximally to achieve. Hout and Morgan (1975) would probably agree. If fear of success does exist, perhaps it could be mitigated at the high school level.

Richard L. Simpson (1974), in a striking survey of 22,000 high school teachers, found evidence that supports the conclusion that teachers may be reinforcing "appropriate sex" roles in an indirect manner. He found that teachers accord prestige to each other on the basis of whether or not they teach sex-typed subjects. His results were clear and consistent. Teachers said they would have more respect for a man teaching high school algebra than a woman and a woman teaching fifth grade than a man. In terms of high school subjects, 53 percent of the respondents accorded the most prestige to a man teaching science, the second highest prestige rank was accorded to a woman teaching English, followed by a man teaching math, a woman teaching a language, and, finally, the least amount of prestige was accorded to a man or a woman teaching in social studies. This suggests that the highest prestige group was conformist men who taught science and the lowest prestige group was nonconformist men who taught English. Thus, Simpson concluded that one might speculate that the social norms governing appropriate occupations apply more strongly to men than to women as occupation is traditionally viewed as the principal male role. This can be taken a step further in speculating that teachers may indeed reinforce sex-typed behavior in their students as well as in each other.

Whatever the causes, structural or sociopsychological, or a combination of the two, there is no doubt that girls are emerging from adolescence and high school feeling ambiguous about their future (Cf. Dellas and Gaier, 1975; Rosen and Aneshensel, 1976). This is problematic for a number of reasons, a central one being that many observers feel it is the school's responsibility to do something about it.

Nonetheless, there have been no adequate explanations provided as to why middle class women are not succeeding in the sense that their male cohort seems to be. What variables are lacking? The social stratification system has favored white males and they, in turn, seem to be the group most compliant with the social mechanisms. For example, they seem to respond better than do women to encouragement to succeed. So, what can account for this ambivalence concerning educational and occupational aspirations in adolescent and post-adolescent girls and women?

Peter Blau and Otis Duncan proposed a paradigm for status attainment in men. It included such variables as soical origins (socioeconomic status), early achievement behavior (for example, academic performance), and encouragement for status achievement from important people (significant others) which would be equated with personal characteristics such as mental ability. Taken together these variables would help to form adolescent attitudes with regard to level of educational and occupational aspirations which would ultimately determine the actual level of education and occupation that a man could expect to attain. W. H. Sewell and A. O. Haller (1969) formulated the "Wisconsin Model" for status attainment based on Blau's and Duncan's paradigm. William Falk and Arthur Cosby (1975) presented this model in block diagram form (see Figure 1) in order to discuss how well the model could explain educational and occupational achievement in women. They found that its explanatory ability, when applied to women, was almost nil.

They concluded that a review of occupational choice theories shows them to be biased toward males, which supports Hout's and Morgan's (1975) findings, and essentially inadequate in their ability to handle factors which influence the occupational choices of women. In addition, Falk and Cosby found that the Wisconsin Model for status attainment revealed a lack of sensitivity to the potential contingencies for women. For example, they discovered that marriage and fertility plans were at least as important as the variables proposed for male achievement in determining the level of educational and occupational attainment to which women would aspire (see Figure 2).

Thus the problem with all of the previous hypotheses concerning achievement motivation (educational and occupational aspiration) in women is that *they do not take into account the social mandate for marriage and motherhood which women are realistically considering as they formulate their educational and occupational objectives.* Perhaps high school girls are not so ambivalent after all. Perhaps they have a very clear idea about their lifelong goals.

College Women Today and Yesterday

If anything, the marriage and motherhood mandate grows stronger by the time a woman enters college. Ann Parelius (1975), using two samples, one in 1969 and the other in 1973, compared college women's views on feminism. She found that in 1973, women were more committed to the *idea* of feminism but in fact *their own personal educational and career*

FIGURE 1

THE WISCONSIN MODEL IN BLOCK DIAGRAM FORM*

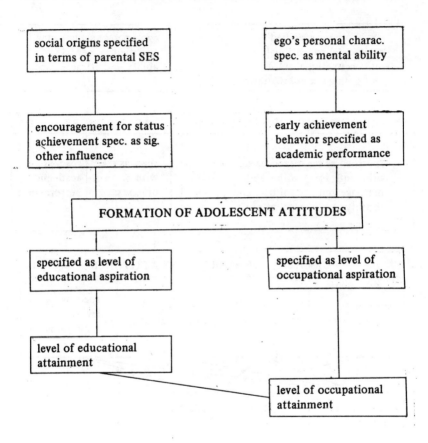

*Source: William W. Falk and Arthur G. Cosby, "Women and the Status Attainment Process," *Social Science Quarterly,* 1975, 56, 2, September, p. 307-314.

FIGURE 2

AN EXPANDED STATUS ATTAINMENT MODEL INCORPORATING
STATUS CONTINGENCIES FOR WOMEN IN BLOCK DIAGRAM FORM*

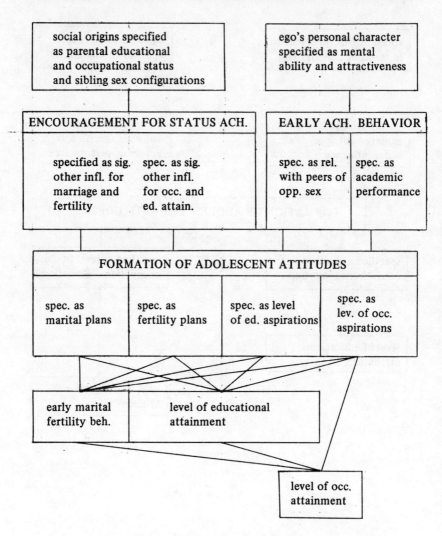

*Source: William W. Falk and Arthur G. Cosby, "Women and the Status Attainment
Process," *Social Science Quarterly*, 1975, 56, 2, September, p. 307-314.

goals had not changed nearly as radically as their outlooks. In other words, there was no decrease in the amount of interest they had in marriage and in motherhood. The idea that was new was the idea of combining marriage, family and a career in a *"double track" pattern.*

All these investigators report that at least 96 percent of female college students want to marry. These figures soar as high as 99 percent in some studies (Cf. Angrist and Almquist, 1975:57; Klemmack and Edwards, 1973). Approximately 94 percent of those wishing to marry also want to have children.

One study reports that of the college women who wish to marry, 77 percent place the role of career before that of housewife, yet they still perceive the routines of career, marriage and family as compatible (Cf. Klemmack and Edwards, 1973).

Even though college women hold strong feminist attitudes, they are ambiguous about their occupational futures in the same way as high school girls. Apparently the social mandate for motherhood (Cf. Zellman, 1976) did not significantly lose force in the 1970s. The attitudes of college women do not correspond with their behavior. That is, although they aspire to careers, they tend not to have realistic plans as to how to meet their aspirations (Cf. Cummings, 1977). Additionally, 35 percent still end up seeing themselves as housewives at the end of their college careers (Cf. Angrist and Almquist, 1975).

In sum, though explanations of women's lack of achievement have been plentiful, ranging from notions of lack of successful role models (Cf. Almquist and Angrist, 1971; Bacon and Lerner, 1975; Douvan, 1976; Ferber and Huber, 1975; Franswa, 1974; Kinnane and Bannon, 1964; Kirschner, 1973; Mackie, 1976; Oliver, 1975; Vogel, et al., 1970, Mayes, 1977) to the reinforcement of traditional roles in schools and textbooks (Cf. Williams, Bennet and Best, 1973; Dellas and Gaier, 1975; Mayes, 1977; Roby, 1976; Simpson, 1974), to the Chameleon Syndrome, whereby girls have been found to be highly adaptable and flexible (Cf. Rosen and Aneshensel, 1976), *the most obvious explanation for women's lack of achievement in early adulthood and throughout life is,* of course, *anticipation of or engagement in marriage, childbearing and childrearing and the time constraints involved therein.*

We should be careful when we allude to "social changes" which, on the surface, appear to separate the 1950s from the 1970s, for example. Perhaps there is much less change than we thought, particularly with regard to women and plans for marriage and fertility. The primary change is that controlled fertility has emerged as a social norm (Cf. Tien, 1967). Attitudinally, this factor separates young college women from the "re-entry women" of today who, for the most part, attended college in the 1950s for the first time.

The Drive to Marry: Competition or Combination?   Women, like men, enter college with their fair share of career aspirations. During the freshman year, most women claim that they would prefer to marry after graduation in order to complete their degrees. Yet, with each successive year, the desire to marry becomes more immediate (Cf. Angrist and Almquist, 1975; Klemmack and Edwards, 1973). The ideal age that is perceived as the right time to marry becomes younger with each passing year. By the time they are seniors, most women would like to find a husband as soon as possible. Nevertheless, each year women become more egalitarian in their views toward marital sex roles. Toward the end of college, women today begin to stress advanced degrees as well as marriage and a kind of ambivalence sets in. Only 16 percent of women attending college for the first time in the 1970s ended up seeing themselves as career women. As previously mentioned, over a third still viewed themselves as housewives (Cf. Angrist and Almquist, 1975). Many of these women, including the housewife-oriented women, expressed their desire to work but they would not take a job that would undermine their husband's pride. The net result is that, if these women were predisposed toward a career, they chose a career in a "safe" female profession. Although there are undoubtedly other reasons why women choose female occupations, it is certain that most of the rationale is based on the realistic expectation that they will have varying responsibilities governed by family commitments.

Thus with regard to educational and occupational attainment, we can clearly see the accuracy of Falk's and Cosby's (1975) expanded model for status attainment which takes into account marital and fertility plans. Since the average woman marries at about age twenty-two and bears her first child within a year and a half after marriage, it is obvious how educational and career plans may be undermined by marriage and the responsibilities that entails.

Of the women in the present study, not fewer than 20 percent dropped out of college to marry. For most of these women, the idea of career was not even a consideration at the time they initially entered college. In fact, for many, the initial motivation to go to college may well have focused on hopes of finding a potentially successful husband who might be able to provide a high standard of living for the family while they, the women, concentrated on raising their children.

For the women interviewed, the average age at first marriage was 20.9. Thirty-three women (73 percent of the total number interviewed) had been to college before their marriage. Of these, eleven were able to attain degrees. This is only one third of the number who attended college. The remainder left school in order to have children, to work to help support their families or for health reasons.

Even the career behavior of these women's mothers did not seem to affect their desire to marry. Eighteen had mothers who worked, but only eight of these women obtained degreees, ten did not. Only three of the women whose mothers worked were career-oriented. Further, it is interesting to note that 40 percent of the "reentry women" were working at clerical jobs before marriage. Most were just biding their time until they married.

Marriage, in and of itself, became the desired goal. As one woman stated: "It just seemed like the thing to do. That's what young people did. You got married and you had kids. [It was] part of the package."

It seems apparent that there was, and is, no real cognitive dissonance among college women with regard to the roles they would play in their adult lives. Many researchers have used sociopsychological variables such as "role-conflict" to explain the "changes" in women's perceived or expected commitments but researchers who have tested this hypothesis on college women do not find data that support the idea.

Barbara Turner and Castellano Turner (1975) assumed that white college women would feel discriminated against by the structure of the occupational system and would therefore suffer from cognitive dissonance. Although their hypothesis did hold true for minorities, they were surprised at the results they obtained for white women. They found that college freshmen who were career-oriented also expected a primary lifetime involvement with home and family. There was no question that these two roles would be combined. In addition, these college women had a strong internal locus of control and attitudes which were consistent with the ideology of individualism. They felt that if they had enough merit, they would have no trouble. In addition, they reported a great deal of parental encouragement for higher education. Their own educational and occupational aspirations were high, but the career-oriented women did not have higher expectations for occupation than the non-career-oriented.

The career-oriented women also had parents of a higher educational status.

So, *career choice for college women,* today and yesterday, *must be accounted for in terms of the total life style which women expect to incur, particularly with regard to marriage.*

For all forty-five women in the present study there was no doubt that being a housewife would comprise the major role complex of their adult lives and at least twenty-nine of these women never considered the pros and cons of having children. They assumed the children would naturally come as a result of the marriage. Therefore, at least initially among this group, there was not a strong desire to work outside of the home. Yet many of them (n=14 or 31 percent) thought that they would pursue careers at some time later in the marriage, that is, after the children were somewhat grown up and could take care of themselves or at least after the children entered school. Nearly one third sought deferred careers.

They differ from career-oriented college women today who have a strong desire to combine the roles of motherhood and career simultaneously. It appears that reentry women are caught as firmly in the current trend toward career as young college women are, particularly with regard to this double track pattern. That is to say, it seems to have become fashionable only recently for women of all ages to be concerned with career pursuits. Most of the women in the present study never thought about a career at all until their children were approaching school age or later. Perhaps this is illustrative of Ross Stolzenberg's and Linda Waite's (1977) "Learning Hypothesis," which states that women learn about the labor market and their potential place within it as they age. Regardless of whether the reasons are economic or for "self-fulfillment," career is very important among today's college women, whether they be young or old. Three-fourths of the women we interviewed were pursuing careers at the time of the interview.

At this point, it seems in order to speculate that variables akin to this Learning Hypothesis which would explain the potential for deferred careers among women should probably be added to the models for women's status attainment in the form of "family stage," "education attained later in the marriage," "divorce," "widowhood," and so on.

Borrowed Status   We have seen that women, whether they have had college experience or not, want husbands. Unfortunately, it is true that women's chances of finding a husband will be lessened if they continue their educations beyond a bachelor's degree. In discussing trends in educational homogamy and marriage, Richard Rockwell (1976) and John Scanzoni (1976) note that women "marry up" whereas men do not. This seems to be a cultural pattern in our country which is at least as strong today as it was in 1910 (Cf. Rockwell, 1976). Education is a major factor in determining mate selection and a major discriminating characteristic in American society. Ann Parelius (1975a) and Joseph Fichter (1972) have determined that many college women feel that obtaining advanced degrees will lessen their chances of finding husbands. They see men as inherently conservative and, according to Rockwell, they are probably right.

In many instances, women consciously limit their education, and they expect to take on the same status and prestige accorded to their husbands by virtue of his educational and occupational status. Thus it has not been so important for them to concentrate on furthering their own educational and occupational aspirations for the purpose of attaining status in society. All they have needed to do is to choose a man who has the particular status or potential status to which they aspire. This model of vicarious achievement through husbands' successes has been called the "borrowed status" model of attainment.

All of the women interviewed assumed that they would share their husbands' status. Eighty-nine percent (n=40) felt that a primary goal in marriage would be to provide emotional support for their husbands. Only nineteen women (42 percent) felt they would work, however, seven of these nineteen qualified their desire to work by stating that they only desired to work while their husbands were in school. One said she would work after the children were in school and two claimed they would work only if it were absolutely necessary to the family's survival that they do so. In fact, it seemed to be expected that women would work in order to help their husbands attain the amount of education they desired while the wives' desires were not even considered. Said one woman:

> When we were at _____ State, they gave diplomas to the women—Ph.T.—when the men got their Ph.D.'s. This was to frame along with his Ph.D. That's how indoctrinated that age group was— to put all your eggs in one basket. Everything was for the man returning from war to the point where the college gave certificates to the wives. Ph.T. Yeah, Pushed Husband Through.

In the beginning, at least, borrowed status seemed to be sufficient to satisfy these women's desires to achieve. Even at the time of the interview, when they were back in college and on career tracks of their own, they still felt that their status coincided with that of their husbands'. In fact, most of the married women in the sample enjoyed annual incomes of $25,000.00 or more at the time of the interview. For the divorced women, the picture was not so bright. So, not only do they borrow their husbands' status, but, as we shall observe later, the economic costs of refusing to ride on the husband's prestige are high.

However, it should be noted that borrowed status may itself be a myth. Ann Oakley (1974) quotes a study carried out in 1969 by Haavio-Mannila which concludes that the ranking of "wife" or "housewife" is low relative to other occupations which appears to suggest that there exists stratification within the family unit when a "normal" family unit exists. Yet, whether myth or reality, women construct their futures around the idea of borrowed status.

Marriage and Mobility   Though marriage may be a boon in terms of women's vertical social mobility, the impairment of women's spatial mobility can present grave consequences.

Saul Feldman (1973) studied the meaning of marriage in terms of mobility for college men and women, particularly with regard to graduate school. He found that women's spatial mobility subsequent to marriage severely limits their alternatives. Rather than selecting graduate schools on the basis of merit, women select graduate schools based on geographical proximity. They also seek jobs in their geographical vicinity.

In the present sample, though thirty-eight out of forty-five women had to relocate at some point or other to follow their husbands' careers, not one family relocated to follow the wife's career. When asked if they would have had to relocate if they wanted to pursue the field they studied in college, only two said yes. One of these decided she would use her career to "fall back on" only in the event of an emergency and the other "gave it up for domesticity." The rest either chose fields which would not demand relocation or they did not choose a field at all, but relied on their husbands' careers.

Many of these women claimed that they had only gone to college in the first place for "enrichment" or to "find a husband." In fact, most of them felt that the question was irrelevant.

Barbara Turner and Joanne McCaffrey (1974) found that college women generally fall into three groups: 1) women who expect and prefer full-time careers to homemaking, 2) women who both expect and prefer homemaking and 3) women who expect homemaking but prefer more outside involvement. They called the third group "frustrated careerists" and claimed that this group is most likely characterized by a high degree of external control and low freedom of movement.

In light of the latent career pursuits of the women in the present study, it seems likely that most of them would fall into a "latent frustrated careerist" pattern with regard to their college participation.

Given that the average age at marriage of these women was only twenty-one, it is safe to say that many of them did not have time to decide on directions for careers before they were married even if they had wanted to pursue careers. As it turns out, however, most of them did not. Many never declared a major. Those who did usually changed majors at least once. They were not highly motivated as a group, nor were they highly committed.

Nonintellectual Factors of Attrition   We have seen that women are less mobile and more likely to drop out than men are. Saul Feldman (1973) found that married women students, particularly in graduate school, are under greater pressure to drop out than male students. They are less likely to stay in graduate school and more likely to perceive emotional stress as the primary deterrent to completing graduate work (Cf. Holmstrom and Holmstrom, 1974). A pattern that seems to be emerging for women graduate students is the perception of stress as they try to combine the routines of graduate school and homemaking, followed by attrition or divorce and then a greater commitment to the homemaker or student role (Cf. Feldman, 1973).

Female graduate students generally have a lower degree of commitment to their studies if they are married. Richard Warnecke (1973) and Laurel Oliver (1975) have both studied women's educational and occupational patterns in terms of commitment and found it to be much lower than that of males in similar positions. Both investigators see this lack of commitment as a function of marriage or plans for marriage. As mentioned before, 20 percent of our sample dropped out of college to marry and only eleven were able to obtain college degrees. Fourteen women (31 percent) had vague plans of pursuing a career at some later period in the marriage. Our small sample, then, adds weight to Saul Feldman's conclusion.

Where Are the Role Models or Why Do They Not Count?   Perhaps these women would not have been so ready to leave school for marriage if they had had more role models. The complaint that women have few successful female mentors abounds in the sociological literature. Elizabeth Almquist and Shirley Angrist (1971) found that career-salient college students are strongly influenced by college professors and occupational role models as compared to non-career-salient college students who are influenced by peers, and family members. In addition, the former perceive their professors and occupational role models as having a more positive evaluation of their academic performance. With regard to background variables, they usually have had more exposure to a greater variety of jobs and they are likely to have working mothers. In contrast, the non-career-salient are more likely to be attached (engaged or having a steady boyfriend), have mothers more actively involved in leisure pursuits and have a more positive perception of their parents' characteristics. Almquist and Angrist concluded that career salience appears to be a function of having a number of reference groups which encourage the pursuit of a career.

In this study, the women's mothers had no significant effect on their daughters' aspirations toward careers, but what about this variable of attachment? Of the thirty-three women who had gone to college, seventeen were in college when they met their husbands and over half of these dropped out to marry. Others dropped out to go to work, or to help work a husband's way through school. Most of these women had had a marginal postion in the college communication patterns as evidenced by their lack of commitment.

Tove Thagaard reports that women in general tend to occupy marginal positions in colleges (1975). It is well established that the informal contact with peers and teachers in the college setting helps to foster attitudes of career salience. Most studies find that women also tend to underestimate their academic performance at the college level, thus, underestimation of ability appears to be a continuing pattern for women from grade school on.

One explanation of these patterns is that there actually are very few female role models in the academic setting. Women's professors are likely to be males and, in their studies, they probably run across very few references to successful women.

Betty F. Kirschner (1973), in a small scale study of ten introductory sociology texts, found that the analysis of women's roles was left "impressively unexplored." Many of the texts failed to index a reference to women. Half of the texts referred to the structure of the American family as basically egalitarian and none of the rest presented a systematic analysis of factors which might contribute to inequality within the family.

However, this may be the least of the college women's problems. A comprehensive study by Lewis Solmon (1973) compares the proportions of women and men in faculty positions over the past century. He found that women hold one-fifth of faculty postions in colleges and universities today *compared with one-third in 1870*. Thirty-three percent of these women are instructors, 20 percent assistant professors, 15 percent associate professors and 9 percent full professors. Clearly, women are found predominantly at the lower ranks and these women are mainly concentrated in smaller and less prestigious institutions.

In comparing proportions of men to women taking doctoral degrees since 1920, Solmon reported the data shown in Table 2.1.

TABLE 2.1

GENDER BREAKDOWN OF PROPORTION OF DOCTORAL
DEGREES TAKEN BY DECADE*

Year	Men	Women
1920	84.3%	15.7%
1930	84.9%	15.1%
1940	86.9%	13.1%
1950	90.5%	9.5%
1960	89.3%	10.7%
1970	86.5%	13.5%

*Source: Lewis C. Solomon, "Women in Doctoral Education, Clues and Puzzles Regarding Institutional Discrimination," *Research in Higher Education*, 1973, 1, 4, pp. 299–332.

The marginal position of women in academe has been noted by Jessie Bernard (1974), Victoria Schuck (1974) and Lorna Jaffe (1973). These researchers have also recognized institutional discrimination against women.

Whether due to marginality or outright discrimination, even though attitudes among college women appear to be changing, particularly in the last decade, there is little evidence that their academic behavior is changing to any great extent relative to their male counterparts. This is interesting with regard to the fact that women take one-half of all bachelor's degrees,

40 percent of all master's degrees and 14 percent of all doctoral degrees (Cf. Fichter, 1972). Perhaps women do not view education as the vehicle to a career in the sense that men do. For women, in light of the strong marital contingency, the path to a career may not be clear cut. In fact, this contingency may explain, at least in part, the reason why women are more likely to change majors in college and are less likely to develop long range career strategies than men (Cf. Epstein in Kundsin, 1973). Choosing a female field is generally more compatible with family activities. That is, female fields do not generally require education beyond the baccalaureate level, they require less on-the-job training, and perhaps they are easier to move in and out of when family responsibilities so demand.

It is possible that women to some extent are being conditioned to perceive the notion of career in an entirely different manner from the way it is perceived by men. This idea is supported by the encouragement from "new" women's magazines such as *Working Woman* and *Working Mother* for women to conceptualize their jobs as careers, no matter what type of occupation they have.

A Brief Introduction to
the Horatia Alger Syndrome in College Women

When Laurie Davidson Cummings (1977) studied college women, she found that they perceived the notion of career as "fulfilling an enjoyable job outside of the home." For the college women she studied, this did not necessarily imply any expected or required commitment or timetable for progression in a career. The feminist women in her sample were more likely to see education as a priority and they were more likely to want to go to work as soon as possible after a child was born. (There was no doubt even among the most feminist women that a child would be born!) Nevertheless, the feminist women were no more likely than any of the other women to have plans as to how to achieve these goals of combining marriage, motherhood and career.

The Horatia Alger model (Cummings, 1977) is based on the idea of merit, which is consistent with Turner's and Turner's (1975) findings, and luck: struggling upward with a benevolent sponsor. These women saw a nonproblematic future as long as they could find a supportive husband.

Clearly, there are a number of problems with this new "feminist" outlook. It promotes individualism, focuses on tokenism and ignores the real structural limitations that women might have to face while in pursuit of a career. Discrimination against women and the idea that most careers require one person to work and another to maintain the home environment (the "two-person career") are examples of the type of structural barriers that can limit women's success (Cf. Papenek, 1973).

The Role of Technological Change

There are changes, however, which would seem to contribute to women's advancement. One overriding factor has significantly altered the picture: more effective methods of birth control. Middle class women now enjoy a longer lifespan, and increased control over the processes of reproduction, and childbearing and childrearing are now concentrated into a shorter segment of the life cycle. The implication of this changing pattern is that women now have more time in the life cycle to work and to pursue that work seriously and continuously. By the time their children are leaving the nest, women today are probably about forty years old. This could leave them potentially thirty years to work.

Further, technical advancements are doing away with differences between men and women with regard to production in the work force, access to education has become more equitable, and marriage is being threatened by increasing liberal attitudes in which the right to earn a living wage and the right to work have become elements. Changes in the composition of the work force, size of family and the structure of education have begun to alter the importance of the function of socialization in the family and this has led to a deemphasis on the psychosocial functions of the family (Cf. Mitchell, 1973).

Taken together, these technological advancements may have a direct effect on women's participation in production. They may also have a direct effect on the future of the family.

The next chapter delves further into the life cycle of the family as it presently exists and women's roles as a member of that dynamic entity.

3
Women's Adult Life Stages: Engaging in the Practices of Motherhood, Disengaging from a Role of Cultural Potency

In chapter 2, we saw that women's educational and occupational aspirations cannot be divided from their aspirations to marry and produce children. They expect, upon marriage, to enter into obligations which will affect their participation in the paid labor force. Thus women often procrastinate in making career or work choices until after marriage. Even feminist-oriented college women today desire to marry whether or not they intend to have children, and, if they do aspire to a career, they hope that their husbands will act as "benevolent sponsors" so that they may reach their goals while continuing their involvement, in a traditional sense, with their families. Because women often delay their entry into the labor force, women's occupational achievements have been examined as a function of women's relationships with men and children.

These relationships also form the basis for analyzing the life cycle of the family. As Paul Glick (1976) points out:

> The life cycle of the family is a term that has been used for many years in reference to the succession of critical stages through which the typical family passes during its life span. This concept provides a highly meaningful framework for the analysis of data in conjugal

families as they pass through such stages as marriage, birth of children, children leaving home, the "postchildren" or "empty nest" period, and ultimate dissolution of the marriage through death of one of the spouses.

The life stages of women who marry and have children are indivisible from the life cycle of the family. Therefore women's work in the labor market is oftentimes dependent on their roles in the home during each family stage. The critical stages in the life of the family become the critical stages in women's lives.

In order to illustrate this point and further define the critical points in women's lives, let us examine the adult life cycles of the mothers who participated in the present study.

Just Before Marriage

When asked "What did you do during your day before you were married?" one woman responded in the following way:

> I was working at a full-time job. It was secretarial work. I worked right up until I was married. At that time, being young and single, footloose and fancy free, I just did things like shopping, going to movies and lunches and playing around.

Another provided this answer:

> I was working at a clerical job immediately before I got married. I had worked for a couple of years after I got out of high school before I got married. I socialized with my future husband and some friends about my own age but I didn't have any real purposeful activity of any sort that I can recall.

Forty-two percent of the women were working at full-time jobs just prior to marriage. A small number of these had been to college or were attending night school, but these were the exceptions to the rule. Three-fourths of the working women (n=19) were engaged in clerical occupations. Many of these clerical workers were relying on typing or shorthand courses they had taken in high school to qualify them for employment.

> It was during the war and my future husband had enlisted so he could go to college for a year . . . I took a business course in high school. There were four children in my family, three girls and a boy, and they had enough money to send one to college. Coming from that long ago, the boy was to go, regardless of whether the other three were better or not. So, really, the decision was made

when I was thirteen. If you weren't to go to college, you took this course . . . My high school placed me in a job . . . When I took my job, there wasn't an opening for typing or shorthand so they put me on a mimeograph machine and after eight months I kept continually saying, "I'm losing my speed." You must use that or you lose it. And I was underpaid and that was not what I had taken the four years in high school to do so I went in to ask to be removed from that position to take a job where I could use that; however, I couldn't find a job so I knew I'd better quit . . . I got a job as a switchboard operator. I was eighteen years old and I just didn't feel I was going anyplace so I stayed in that job until I was married.

"I wasn't going anyplace." This statement exemplifies the feelings of the majority of the clerical workers before marriage. This population focused on marriage and family as the predominant goal of adult life.

Fifty-one percent (n=23) of the women interviewed were full-time students before marriage. Very few of these were able to obtain degrees. Of the forty-five, thirty-three had been to college at some point prior to marriage, but only twenty-three of these mentioned college as their major activity immediately before marriage. Of the number who had been to college, eleven had managed to obtain degrees. Most of these degrees were associate's degrees. Whether the women earned degrees or not, the primary drive was toward marriage and motherhood.

I was in school before I was married. I had gone from high school to college and the only kind of work that I had done was on the ranch where I grew up. I had a scholarship to a teacher's college in elementary ed. Elementary ed was what I was in mainly because that was what my mother wanted me to be in and that was the only way out . . . I did a lot of church work. I very much enjoyed square dancing and playing cards. I didn't socialize very much because I lived off campus. I met my husband at a church retreat and married nine months later.

There was no shortage of elementary education majors of those who were in college:

I was in college. I was a sophomore in college when I got married. At that point, I was in elementary education and art. I was just really involved in school and with friends. That was my full-time activity. I spent a lot of time with my future husband. We got married at school during Christmas break and I started to go to school part-time. I had flunked out of school, really . . . I had been

> doing too much partying . . . My husband continued full-time and his grades improved immensely and he graduated after a year. After he graduated, I never took another class.

Even before marriage, these women were lending financial, as well as emotional, support to their future husbands:

> I went to two years at the university and then I dropped out to work before we married for financial reasons. I did secretarial and book-keeping work. I worked for two years after we were married until my child was born.

Seventeen women were in college when they met their husbands and ten of these dropped out to marry (see chapter 2).

The remainder of the women married just after graduation from high school and one woman's parents signed papers so she could marry while still in high school.

Thus, even before marriage took place, for most of these women it was already established that they would be the adaptable partners in the marriage. They would adjust their goals and desires to conform to the demands of husbands' jobs and educations and children's needs. Before marriage, most of them held low paying jobs or half-heartedly pursued a college education. One-fifth of the entire sample had dropped out of college specifically to marry, and, as we have seen, career was not a consideration at this point. Rather, their future husbands' careers and educations were of the utmost concern. By the age of twenty, most of these women had already developed the classical "other orientation," designing one's activities to meet others' needs, which characterizes the stereotype of traditional women's roles in the family. All of the women in the present study knew that being a housewife would comprise the major role complex of their adult lives.

Becoming a Housewife

In describing women's adult life stages, Helena Lopata (1971) began with marriage. She referred to this point as "Becoming a Housewife." This seems logical with regard to the fact that women who work thirty hours a week in the paid labor market still report spending thirty-four hours a week on housework (Cf. Angrist and Almquist, 1975). Upon marrying, middle class women tend to believe that their first responsibility will be to bear and raise children and maintain the home environment. These activities span the adult life cycle.

The second stage Lopata mentions is the "Expanding Circle Stage" which begins when the first child is born and ends with the birth of the second. The third stage is the "Peak Stage" when two or more children are preschool age. The "Full House Plateau" is the fourth stage which occurs when childbearing has been completed. This is followed by the "Shrinking Circle Stage" which begins when the first child leaves home and ends with the departure of the last child from the home. The final stage is the "Minimal Circle Stage." This pattern is still widely accepted by social researchers as the most descriptive representation of the female adult cycle, and, indeed, the women in the present study tend to picture their own lives in the terms that these stages describe. We will explore each of these stages, in turn, relying on the life histories of the women interviewed for this study. The ages during the various life stages of these women are contained in Table 3.1.

TABLE 3.1

STAGE IN LIFE CYCLE OF REENTRY WOMEN
AT THE TIME THEY WERE INTERVIEWED

Stage	*Age Range*	*Average Age*	*Number of Women*
Expanding Circle	27–37	30.75	4
Peak Stage & Full House Plateau	31–41	35.64	25
Shrinking Circle	42–52	45.0	7
Minimal Circle	43–60	52.88	8

Age at Marriage   In the present study, the average age at marriage or Becoming a Housewife was 20.9. The eighty year average in the United States for marriage between 1900 and 1980 has also been 20.9, so, in this regard, the women were directly in line with the national average. The median age at first marriage has varied somewhat from decade to decade, however, with the highest level at 21.4 years during the decade from 1900–1910 and the lowest level at 20.0 for those who married during the 1950s (Cf. Glick, 1976). Paul Glick (1976) states that women of this decade not only had the youngest marriages but also the smallest proportion of women who never married occurred in this decade. This number was about 4 percent. This decade also saw the highest birth rate for many years. Thus marriage and motherhood were expected life events for almost all women of marriageable age during the 1950s. At least one-fourth of the women in the present study fall into this age cohort.

Upon Becoming a Housewife, the women's activities often underwent dramatic changes, from moving to new states, to going to work, to putting husbands through school, to becoming mothers immediately.

> My activities changed drastically when I got married because right after getting married I started school. My husband had been at the school working on a degree before we were married. I quit working and moved to the university town. We left the university when he graduated. I never was able to finish my degree. We moved away from that town when he got his first job out of college. I started working for a publishing company until I got pregnant and I quit working at six months pregnant. I got concerned about getting my nursery in order and buying all these little clothes. I wanted to be home and play the role, I guess.

No matter what the women did, they oriented their lives around their husbands' and, at times, this became confusing because the changes were so sudden. In general, the husbands continued to do whatever they were doing before marriage. It was the wives who changed to accommodate the marriage, changes which sometimes resulted in confusion:

> I remember being bewildered by the whole thing when I was first married. I thought, "What the hell is going on here?" . . . I hadn't realized how much he drank and I was seeing it every night. I had this sort of confusion in my mind from the first. I was a very typical housewife. I'd get all the breakfast stuff done and get off and go to work and come back and clean the house and all that sort of thing. And weekends I was really lost because he was working. He worked on the weekends and it seemed like he was gone a lot and when I got married I just quit everything. I wasn't in school and I didn't belong to anything and I had nothing to do on the weekends when he was gone and I felt kind of isolated. I just sort of waited around. And then we made friends but it was the wife of the guy that he knew that became my friend, you know, and we got into some organizations but it was all small talk. At that time I worked as a secretary full-time.

It was expected that the women would adapt.

I didn't work when I first got married. We were living in a small mountain town for the first two months and then the next three we were living in a very small town in another state. But I didn't work outside the home. I just did the housework. I did a lot of needlepoint and they had a gift shop where I lived and I sold a lot of needlework through that gift shop. That was the first five months of marriage. Then we came back here to the town where we started and moved in with his mother. He got part-time jobs, nothing permanent, but we took the plunge and bought the lot and built the first section of the house ourselves. Then he got a full-time job and I was building the house.

For all of these women, marriage was the object of their youths regardless of education or work history, and woe unto the woman who was not married by the time she was twenty-two:

I had completed a B.A. in sociology before I met my husband. I met him about two weeks after I graduated. But when I actually graduated without a man, back in those days, it was terrible. If I'd only known then that I was going to meet someone two weeks later . . . In those days it was really traumatic if you hadn't caught a man before graduation.

Initial Relocation Patterns   Women adjust. Part of that initial adjustment to marriage often includes relocating, which, in many cases, is a condition of marriage in the first place. We have seen the sort of problems which arise with restricted spatial mobility with regard to educational or career pursuits, but what effect does marriage, in and of itself, have on women's place of residence?

Fifty percent of the women relocated to follow their husbands' jobs. Because they felt uprooted by the move, the women sought to become involved in their new surroundings. They joined bowling leagues, gave Tupperware parties, volunteered work in local hospitals, socialized with their husbands' colleagues, took up church activities, redecorated houses and took tennis lessons.

Nine women relocated upon marriage to go to the towns where their husbands attended college. The following statement typifies many women's experiences:

I married my husband nine months after we met. We married on his vacation from school between semesters. We moved then and I transferred to his school. I took typing and shorthand and then I transferred to his school. I took typing and shorthand and then I dropped out. Then I worked at various jobs until he got through school. He took a job in a small town and we moved there and he didn't like it and quit so we moved again.

The women who relocated to follow their husbands to school comprise about one quarter of the sample.

Many women went to work, but the (often multiple) moves forced them into occupations which they could easily move in and out of. We have already heard from the woman who did needlepoint and sold it. In fact, she did not refer to this as work since it was accomplished in the home. Another made and sold quilts. Arts and crafts become important skills in making extra money.

Becoming a Housewife and Paid Work   More important than arts and crafts, however, was to keep those typing skills polished. In all, forty-two out of forty-five women worked after marriage and two-thirds of these worked off and on at clerical jobs. Though these women may have worked up to thirty-five years after marrying, very few of them saw their own work as important. They saw their own work as important only insofar as it helped their husbands get through school.

I saw my work as a comptometer operator as vital so my husband could get through school. I mean it was every bit as important as him going to school every day. As I say I've always felt, and I think he has too, that marriage is a complementary thing, if one needs to go to school — as we switched going to school — and we did it for the benefit of the marriage and future children. First, I'd go to school and he'd go to work and then he went to work while I got the comptometer training so that I could do that while he went to dental school.

In response to the question, "Did you see your own work as secondary?" the majority of people answered with a succinct "Definitely."

I saw my own work as absolutely secondary to my husband's. I always thought of him as the provider, mainly because I didn't feel qualified for anything, I wasn't even qualified for the work that I did do. I mainly got jobs because I'm an intelligent person but I've had only one year of typing in high school and that was it. Other than that I really wasn't qualified and that made for defeat. It always made me feel insecure in my positions.

Another woman said:

> I have seen my own work as secondary to my husband's. During my first marriage I certainly didn't see my work as significant at all. It was just money coming in to help the family. That's all. I've tried to see my work differently in my second marriage. I don't even know if it's even possible for a man to even realize what it means not to have work. I have an inability sometimes to stand up for myself. So much of my life, I feel I haven't counted. I can't understand anybody seeing that I'm important at all. You have to know inside of yourself that you matter, that you can make a contribution.

In retrospect, many women wondered what they had missed by being relegated to lower positions in the paid work world. However, the initial contracts that they entered into when they took the vows of marriage required that their primary roles be involved with the direction of the household and the bearing and raising of any children which might ensue. Eighty-nine percent felt that a major part of their marital role complex would be to support their husbands emotionally in whatever activities they might undertake, but many drew the line at offering financial support. They were not getting married to work. That was their husband's job. Nearly half stated that they did not intend to support their husbands financially during the marriage. Forty-two percent said they would support their husbands under certain circumstances. Out of these nineteen women (42 percent), seven said that they would only support their husband while he was in school, one said she might work but only after the children were in school and two said they would go to work only if it were necessary.

This woman does a good job of summing up the general feeling:

> I did not expect to have to support my husband after marriage. That was a surprise [when I did]. At the time I was married, the only women who worked were the very few career women and we really—Business women have always looked hard. As women, we didn't really have high regard for them because they were hard. They weren't feminine women. At the time I married, I really felt the only women who worked were widows or those women who had an unfortunate marriage and had a divorce or women who

were married to no-good men. So when I was married, I fully expected that when I worked it was my right of choice and that my money would go to what I wanted it to go to. This was my generation. We worked not because we were supposed to—only if we wanted something nicer than we had. It was not supposed to be an economic necessity. This isn't true anymore.

If the women were pursuing careers before marriage or during early marriage, it was only to have something "to fall back on." They were not committed to education or to other major activities outside of the home.

When the women did hold jobs, they organized them around the demands of their husbands' jobs. Hanna Papanek (1973) found this to be a pattern among women. Further, she maintains that the requirements of the husband's job can probably be seen as a major factor in women's reluctance or inability to develop independent careers (if they are college educated) on a level for which their educations have prepared them. As we have observed, one of the major deterrents to a full-time career for a married woman is likely to be her lack of mobility, resulting in her inability to follow the job market (Cf. Duncan and Perrucci, 1976; Peterson and Peterson, 1975; Hunt and Hunt, 1977).

Even if they do not want or expect to work, 75 percent of women will probably work at some time during marriage (Cf. Young, 1978). It seems logical that, if women do not draw their identity from participation in the labor market, yet must work for pay, conflicts are likely to arise early in their marriages. Douglas Hall (1975) found that tensions between husband and job cause women a great deal of stress during the period of marriage before children are born. This seems to be true particularly for those women, for example, the 50 percent of the present sample, who did not intend to work during marriage, those who saw their primary roles as wife, mother and housewife.

When they found themselves at work it was not at the type of jobs which they considered glamorous or even interesting. It was dull, boring, repetitive work. In addition, to add to their problems, they were often in a new location where they had few friends and few contacts. For many, marriage was not what they had expected. Some were disappointed and they couldn't understand why.

A Matter of Loneliness   The women relocated to follow husbands' jobs. This meant leaving family and friends and the move often entailed a great deal of loneliness for the wives. If a physical move was not in-volved, a "psychological" move often was, as in this woman's case:

I quit working. I quit seeing the majority of my girlfriends at the time [I got married]. I limited myself to my husband's activities and my husband's schedule: working on the car, waxing the car, just staying around the house watching television. In the first place, it was expected that I would stop my activities and I went with the theory that I should and I did.

When asked, what did you do during your day during your early marriage, another woman provided this response:

I kept on working, but it did change my life drastically because I no longer did as I pleased and I tended to be a very iconoclastic kind of person. I did exactly as I pleased, why and where. I was very promiscuous. When I became involved with my husband and sub-sequently married, I did a total reversal. I became very much the little woman and fell into the classical pattern of the subservient wife. My whole life revolved completely around him.

Nearly all of the women gave up the kind of life they had had before marriage. For at least fifteen out of forty-five women, having a baby was an immediate factor which changed their lives upon marriage. One-third of the sample had had babies within the first year of marriage. By the second year of marriage 44 percent had borne their first child.

I worked for awhile. I was pregnant at the time and I was just huge and being pregnant and working and socializing with some of his groups at the college. I worked in a little donut shop and ate all those donuts. It was almost disgusting I could eat so many of the silly things . . . It was a silly little job, just something to do with my time because there was nothing to do. I would say it was a very lonely year. I didn't know any friends that my husband knew because this was his fourth year in college and he knew a lot of people so I would call it a lonely year.

What did you do during your day during your early marriage?

When we got married my life changed drastically. I had to quit working. We moved from California to Oklahoma. I was about six months pregnant when we got married and we lived in Oklahoma for a year. This was hard because I didn't know anybody in Okla-homa and it was kind of hard to change from being active all the time to just barely existing. I mean there was nothing to do. I

couldn't go out anymore. I was just totally tied down . . . To him,
I was just supposed to stay home and take care of my baby and
that was it. For years it was twenty-four hours a day, seven days a
week. No more nothing . . . I just about went goofy.

Loneliness surrounded these newly married women's lives like a shroud.
Marriage was not what they had expected. The marriages these women
entered into were not the marriages they had dreamt about in childhood.

I was still young and I thought that marriage should be roses and
bouquets and all those wonderful storybook things you read about
but I was wrong! Was I ever surprised! I did absolutely nothing.
I quit school. My husband finished up that first year we were married. He was in college and he didn't believe in women going to
school, so there was no reason for me to go to school while he was
finishing up so I became addicted to soap operas and in a tiny
apartment, there's only so much you can clean and so all I did the
rest of my day was watch soap operas and have dinner on the table
when he came home and that was my exciting life. It went on for
a year and a half. Then a friend of mine suggested that I go to
college. My husband was working then and I was even more bored.
I was going crazy. So I enrolled at a university and we fought and
fought over that. I was determined though. Well, he got a transfer
and we moved . . . So I stayed out for another year and then decided
to go back to college again but we argued every morning. He
couldn't understand why I wanted a college education and a degree
but it was a major goal of mine. We fought for a year and a half and
I finally walked out and never came back.

Twenty-one out of forty-five of these first marriages ended in divorce.
The loneliness of being displaced, the strain of having children immediately and the partially coerced, partially agreed upon subservience were
all factors.

Arlene Skolnick (1978) claims that the divorce rate is rising in this
country because so much emphasis is placed on marriage. Marriage is
held up as the answer to all the problems one might encounter in life.
She quotes Philip Slater as saying that in traditional societies:

. . . spouses are not asked to be lovers, friends, and mutual therapists. But it is increasingly true of our society that the marital bond
is the closest, deepest, most important, and putatively most en-
during relationship of one's life. Therefore it is increasingly likely
to fall short of the demands on it and to be dissolved . . .

For the women interviewed in this study who were divorced, this statement seems a very apt description of the intensity with which they savored marriage initially and why they were subsequently disappointed by it. In Lillian Rubin's (1979) study of the "midlife search for self" it is reported that 20 percent of the women she interviewed value their marriages more than they feel their husbands do. For many women, marriage, "Becoming a Housewife," is the goal of adult life. Men have traditionally had other goals as well.

These women unanimously felt marriage to be their primary adult role. They sought to become "junior partners," upholding the traditional stereotypes of women as fulfilling a supportive backstage role, minding the house and children and creating a comfortable home environment (Cf. Press and Whitney, 1971; Lipman-Blumen, 1972).

Only one role could possibly be more important to these women than being a good wife, and that role was being a good mother.

The Expanding Circle Stage

> One of the reasons I got married was to have kids. I knew that. I decided when I was thirteen that I was going to have six boys and that stuck with me and it really was a very strong need and I knew I wanted kids so I had to get married. Marriage and kids are two entirely different things. It is one thing to be married and another to have kids. You know, you take the package deal.

Most of the mothers interviewed had wanted children from the time they were very young. At least twenty-nine women assumed that children would naturally come as a result of marriage. For some, marriage was part of the "package deal" of having children. For others, children were part of the "package deal" of marriage. For all of them, the two went hand in hand. Most of these women did not consciously consider a choice in regard to having children. Children were part of marriage and marriage was what women did.

Some, such as the following woman, found motherhood fulfilling in the early days.

> I quit my job two months after I got pregnant. The seven months there was nothing to do. I got hooked on soap operas and I read but I was all alone. After the baby came, I got the biggest kick out of being a mother. After I got the baby home, it was fantastic. I loved being pregnant. I loved walking around with my big tummy

like I am really something. I was just very contented, especially with the first one.

Others bemoaned their pregnancies:

I dropped out of college to get married. It was very boring when I first got married. He was still in school and it was kind of a shock, being married and not being in school. I mean, I was happy with him but it was – different. I moved to be with him at his school. I did housework . . . fed his friends . . . One of my husband's friends worked for the school radio station and I did some ads for them and then they wanted me to do a women's radio program but I guess I just – At that point, I was pregnant, I guess, and I wasn't sure I wanted to do it and I freaked out. I didn't know where to begin and I didn't know where to turn for help in forming it. My voice would have been okay but I didn't know what to put into it. I hadn't been a housewife that long and that's what they wanted. I got pregnant within the first year after I was married. It was real stupid.

Whether motherhood was seen as a positive or negative experience, there was no doubt for any of the women that it would occur. Usually it was just a matter of time. "I got married in May. I was still in high school – just graduating. I became pregnant right after I was married." And they kept coming: "Jill was born in August of '52, Patrick in February of '54, Lilly in December of '55, Georgia in October of '57. Inside of five years and two months, I had had four children." The average woman in our sample did not have four children, however. Most of the women were content to stop at two. But this was on the low side when compared to the national average. For women bearing children in the 1950s, the national average number of children was 3.1, in the 1960s, 3.4 and in the early 1970s, 3.4 (Cf. Glick, 1976). The average for the period from 1900 to 1980 was 3.3 children per woman. Three point three children demand a lot of time! According to information from the U. S. Bureau of the Census, 90 percent of women over twenty-five are married and 90 percent of those women have children. In the 1950s only 10 percent of women of childbearing age and over, whether married or not, were childless (Cf. Glick, 1976). Even if women do have other plans in addition to marriage and motherhood for their adult lives, their plans for becoming wives and mothers are not significantly altered. In an article supporting voluntary childlessness, J. E. Veevers (1975) opens with the following statement:

The dominant cultural definitions of parenthood indicate that having children are natural and normal behaviors, which constitute religious and civic moral responsibilities, and which reflect sexual competence.

Evidence that strong mores for couples to have children exist in our society has been compiled by A. Stroup (1966), J. E. Veevers (1972, 1973, 1975), Jessie Bernard (1974) and P. Neal Ritchey and C. Shannon Stokes (1974). Women are pressured from all sides to become mothers.

Even if women have other desires or goals, and children may compete with these goals, voluntary childless wives are still considered rare and deviant (Cf. Ritchey and Stokes, 1974; Veevers, 1975; Russo, 1976). Only about 4 percent of wives want no children.

Jessie Bernard (1974) makes the claim that this form of behavior is not logical. Whether a particular individual is predisposed to enjoy the mother role and to do well in it or not, all women must become mothers regardless of anything else they might want to do or wherever their talents and interests lie. She states:

> Some [mothers] are accepting and loving; some are rejecting . . . If we forced every girl to become, say, a librarian or nurse or secretary or what-have-you, we would not be surprised if some performed well and others poorly. Or that some enjoyed their work while others did not. We would recognize that they were all different and that a common career would not be congenial to all. We show no such logic in the case of mothers. We expect every woman not only to want babies but also to love motherhood. If she does not, we make her feel deviant. (p. 31)

Women do become mothers and children do take time.

> With the birth of the first child I stopped working in the seventh month. It seemed like I spent twenty-four hours a day with the baby and a lot of that was my own doing. Looking back on it, I realize I had not had a strong enough sense of myself. I totally lost my personality in being Mommy. So I have been trying to get out of that role ever since. When you have two of them two years apart, you're potty training forever, so to speak.

This woman was twenty-five years old when her first child was born and still she felt unsure. For the women in our sample, the average age at first birth was 23.5 (see Table 3.2). The eighty year national average has ranged decade by decade from 21.5 to 23.5 (Cf. Glick, 1976), so the women in the present study were a little on the old side. Nonetheless, many felt unprepared for the responsibility having children involved and many were overwhelmed by children. A number of women mentioned that they felt the demands of home life foreclosed the possibility of participation in other activites during the time they were young mothers.

TABLE 3.2

AGE OF REENTRY WOMEN DURING IMPORTANT LIFE EVENTS
COMPARED TO THE NATIONAL AVERAGE

Age

Life Event	*Reentry Women*	*National Average**
Marriage	20.9	20.9
Birth of First Child	23.5	22.6
Birth of Last Child	27.5	31.3
First Child Leaves Home	45.0	unknown
All Children Have Left Home	52.0	unknown

*Source of reported national averages: Paul C. Glick, "Updating the Life Cycle of the Family," *Journal of Marriage and the Family,* 1976, 39, 1, February, pp. 5-13.

And, as Bernard (1974) points out, women become mothers regardless of how much training they have in other areas and how little they have in mothering. It is a fact that many women are entering the role completely unprepared:

> I had never been around small children before so I was unsure of myself. I had never been responsible for younger kids. The inexperience left me feeling very uncertain and inadequate. I watched

television a lot. I read fiction a lot and visited with neighbors. I never went the bridge club route. I never had the time—the baby-sitting co-op consumed a lot of time.

The children demanded so much time and there was so much on-the-job training involved, that, by the time the second child was born, nearly all of the women had left the labor force. For the childrearing years, at least, this pattern can easily be applied to the women in this sample. The needs of children generally precluded other major activities.

Most women continued to work only up until the birth of the first child, which fits with trends noted by Shirley Angrist and Elizabeth Almquist (1975) and Glen H. Elder and Richard C. Rockwell (1976). In the Expanding Circle Stage, women institutionalize their "other orientation." Even if they would like to pursue a career or other interests, a strong tension exists between children and career in terms of time and energy constraints and the responsibility a woman feels toward home and family. In 1970, more than half of the women who ceased working in the previous twelve months mentioned home or family responsibilities as the reason (Cf. Lave and Angrist, 1974). In addition, wives who work forty hours a week still report spending twenty-five hours a week on housework (Cf. Zellman, 1976). This implies that when women do take a job outside the home, they are not substituting paid work for housework. Essentially, they are taking on a double work load and the needs of the employer cannot usually be reconciled with the needs of children. Specifically, for the 6,000,000 preschool age children with working mothers, only 641,000 can be accommodated by the existing day care centers (Cf. Zellman, 1976). This is roughly 10 percent of the children of working mothers (Cf. Angrist and Almquist, 1975).

And even without working in the paid labor market, full-time mothering is not an easy task.

The Peak Stage and the Full House Plateau

I had four children. During that span of time, I was gardening. I was canning, freezing, sewing, taking care of the place, you know, the house. I made all of the kids' clothes, drapes . . . Actually, it got to the point where after Lucy went to school, I really wanted to go back to school or back to a job out of the home but I made the statement so many times that my real income was so great that I couldn't afford to go back to work. You see, when you're doing the gardening, the canning, all of this—baking—I made all the bread and everything—so, the real income was so great it was very difficult. I knew I couldn't go back to a lot of jobs and make enough to replace it. Neither could I handle time and energywise a job and what I was doing. There's a limit. Don't have your kids that close together if you want to do anything else.

How Much Time Does it Take?   Though one woman in the sample had her last child at the age of forty-one, the average woman had completed her childbearing period at age 27.6. This was lower than the national average. The average age of women at the birth of their last child has ranged from 32.9 during the first decade of this century to an all-time low of 29.6 in the 1970s (Cf. Glick, 1976). Thus by two and a half years after marriage, the childbearing period had begun and by a little over four years after marriage, childbearing had been completed. Well over half of the women interviewed had completed childbearing but still had all of their children at home at the time of the interview.

The women in this stage, usually the Full House Plateau, when most of the children were school age rather than preschool age, ranged in age from 31 to 41 with an average age of 35.6.

In the Peak Stage and Full House Plateau, women report spending most of their time on housework and childcare. The women in our sample allocated an average of thirty-eight hours a week to housework (see Table 3.3). Time spent on housework ranged from eight to ninety-eight hours a week with those falling at the bottom of the range having help from family members and occasionally hired help, although this was very rare for people in this stage of life. Most did not include childcare in their definitions of housework. Rather, housework was seen as household maintenance.

When childcare is taken into account as a part of housework, women report spending an average of seventy-seven hours a week on housework (Cf. Oakley, 1974). Other studies throughout this century show that women spend not less than fifty-one hours a week doing housework, on the average, and these studies range up to eighty-two (Cf. Oakley, 1974:94).

Regarding childcare, nineteen women in our sample said that they thought it was important for a woman to stay at home with her children. Their advice for mothers was: Stay at home for at least the first year and possibly until the child is eighteen. Most, however, felt that up until age six was enough time. Fourteen people felt it was not important for a mother to stay home with her children, but most of these admitted that this had not always been their opinion. Earlier in their lives, they had been convinced that staying at home with children was what they should be doing.

TABLE 3.3

COMPARISON OF LIFE STAGE AND HOURS
SPENT PER WEEK ON HOUSEWORK

	Number of Hours Spent on Housework	
Stage	*Range*	*Average*
Expanding Circle	4–65	31.25
Peak Stage & Full-House Plateau	8–98	38.12
Shrinking Circle	8–70	40.86
Minimal Circle	4–60	28.86

Thus about two-thirds of the sample was evenly split in terms of feelings about caring for one's own children. The remaining third could not decide. The issue was just too complex, given the mixed messages prevalent in the media today.

Pressure in the Peak Stage   Douglas Hall (1975) found that pressures for women would rise in the Peak Stage. Because there is a great decrease in employment at this stage, work-related pressures are at a minimum, but, in contrast, self-related pressures reach a maximum. The fact that women become most concerned about their own needs just when they are least able to pursue outside interests may suggest that women's self-expression needs are fulfilled, at least in part, through paid work (Cf. Hall, 1975).

From questionnaires returned from 261 people, Hall determined that age, in and of itself had little to do with the role experiences of the women studied. Rather, it was life stage and the number of roles women were performing that had a direct effect on satisfaction, happiness and the perception of pressures and strain. The more advanced the woman's life stage was the less satisfied and happy she was and the more pressures she perceived. The explanation offered was that women felt less potent as time passed.

Hall found that work pressures declined through the Peak Stage and then became more salient in the Full House Plateau and Shrinking Circle Stage. This finding concurs with Lopata's (1971) findings. Self-related pressures tended to increase through the Peak Stage, decrease in the Full House Plateau and increase in the Shrinking Circle Stage. Time constraint pressures which were prevalent did not appear to be related to life stage in Hall's study.

In this study, pressure points discussed in the Peak Stage and Full House Plateau, in order of importance, include the following (where on the average, three of these categories were present simultaneously):

1. Time/Children
2. Marriage or Relationship with Person of the Opposite Sex
3. Self
4. Home
5. Money
6. School

Time, children and marriage were at the top of the list which stands to reason in light of women's activities at this stage.

> I see pressures stemming from time and husband's career decisions. I have to organize my life around his and change it as he changes his career, particularly with the last move. Regarding time, I get interested in so many things and when I get interested it's not superficial. I have to go all out for it and I can't do all the things I want to do.

In contrast to Hall's study, work was rarely mentioned as a pressure point, yet all of the women interviewed in the Peak Stage and the Full House Plateau were beginning a career pursuit. This was generally seen as a point of stimulation, however, rather than a cause of stress. For most, the idea of a career provided a source of satisfaction and self-fulfillment. The pressure came from not enough time to do everything that needed to be done to prepare for a career and to meet family demands. Many people shared the sentiments of this woman:

> My children are eleven and seven — school age. I want to try to find a place in the world. I don't know, it seems very hard these days, but I want to be more flexible. I want to do some life planning

and get some counseling along those lines now. I wish I had done that before I started back to school but now I'm aware of all these things . . . I've just started to not need childcare now which was the big barrier in my life.

The "Learning Hypothesis"   Ross M. Stolzenberg and Linda J. Waite (1977) studied the effect of young women's age on the relationship between their fertility expectations and plans for future labor force participation. They found that work plans have only a marginal effect on the fertility expectations. They attribute this to something they call the Learning Hypothesis which postulates that women learn about the labor market as they age. Stolzenberg and Waite do not go into the reasons why this might be true, if the Learning Hypothesis is indeed a plausible explanation. We have already seen that for most women childbearing is completed by age twenty-nine. Since childcare and household maintenance demand so much time during the Peak Stage and the Full House Plateau, one could speculate that it is unreasonable for most women to consider their labor force participation seriously until the children are at an age where they do not need round-the-clock care. Whereas Stolzenberg and Waite say that if women learn the realities of labor market participation at an earlier age they may have fewer or no children, most research on childbearing would seem to indicate that women will continue to have children and that they will have no fewer children, but that they will try to integrate the demands of children with the demands of work. If they learn about the labor market as they age, it is because participation only becomes feasible when they enter into certain stages of their lives, that is, labor force participation becomes more a reality after all the children have been borne. Women indicate that, at this point, they realize that long-term interruptions in work can be kept to a minimum. At this time, they are in a better position to make a serious commitment.

Most of the women in the present sample were in the Peak Stage or the Full House Plateau when they started thinking about working.

I never really thought about a career as a possible reality until after my last baby was born. I had thought about going back to school and doing something that year when I was pregnant but I don't think it became specific until after he was born.

As previously mentioned, these women grew up believing that their primary adult roles would be involved with marriage and motherhood, so it stands to reason that marriage and motherhood would be the major pressure points during the Peak Stage and the Full House Plateau.

Self-related pressures were usually related to marriage and motherhood. It was usually the case that the women wanted a source of satisfaction and identity outside of marriage, but the pursuit of external goals took time away from marriage and motherhood, which led to a great deal of soul-searching and personal goal assessment. A woman in the throes of this self-related struggle made the following comment:

> Society as a whole is a great pressure. It is the great captor. What I expect of myself is a pressure. This relates to society and what I expect of myself in relationship with my husband and children. It's not that my husband's demanding, because there are certain things he wants of me, but it's what I think I should do. I've led the traditional role of a wife and mother—what you're supposed to do—for so long, it's a little hard to break away.

And her goal was to break away by undertaking activities external to the marriage.

Thus, if boredom and loneliness and the acquisition of a new life style were the causes of women's troubles when Becoming a Housewife and in the Expanding Circle Stage, disrupting the family status quo which took so many years to establish becomes the source of pressure in the Peak Stage and the Full House Plateau.

Concerns and allocation of time undergo even further rearrangements when women enter into the Shrinking Circle Stage.

The Shrinking Circle Stage

When does the Shrinking Circle Stage occur? The stereotyped grandmother is a white-haired old lady who bakes chocolate chip cookies for her grandson who comes to stay for the summer and who has just returned from a day of fishing with his grandpa. But today's grandmothers are not necessarily old or even gray headed. When women bear their last child at twenty-seven, as have many of the women in this study, they will be forty-five when that child is eighteen and probably about forty-nine when their last child has children of her own. At forty-five, women can still expect to live about thirty years.

Essentially what has occurred is that childbearing has been concentrated into a shorter period in the life cycle necessitating that women expect to replace mothering with other activities at mid-life.

Most of the women in the present study perceived that the major role complex involved in motherhood was coming to an end or would be coming to an end in the foreseeable future and all were looking for alternative ways to spend their time. It was not that they had time to kill, however.

In fact, the number of hours spent on housework alone rises slightly for this age group to about forty-one hours a week and home becomes more of a concern than it was for women in the Peak Stage and Full House Plateau. Perhaps spending more hours on housework is an indication that these women, on one level, have succeeded. Family income for this group generally exceeded $30,000.00 for married women. In other words, it is reasonable to expect that these women would be "moving up" socially and living in larger houses as their husbands become more successful in their jobs and careers. Larger houses may mean more housework, regardless of the fact that children may be leaving the home.

Philip Slater reminds us:

> The suburban dweller seeks peace, privacy, nature, community, and a child-rearing environment which is healthy and culturally optimal. Instead he finds neither the beauty and serenity of the countryside, the stimulation of the city, nor the stability and sense of community of the small town, and his children are exposed to a cultural deprivation equaling that of any slum child with a television set . . . A final irony of the suburban dream is that, for many Americans, reaching the pinnacle of one's social ambitions (owning a house in the suburbs) requires one to perform all kinds of menial tasks (carrying garbage cans, mowing lawns, shoveling snow, and so on) that were performed for him when he occupied a less exalted status. (1970:9–10)

Slater's list would not be complete without mentioning cleaning four bathrooms rather than two and a half, a task many women regarded as trying to their patience, to say the least. Some of these women mentioned that they felt like prisoners in their dream houses. A woman who had attained a very stable home environment in the country said:

> I have an insatiable curiosity. I'm very conscious of all the things I don't know and I'm fascinated by so many areas . . . It was really like being in a prison because my husband totally rejected those things I wanted to pursue and there were no outlets for me.

Later, the situation became almost intolerable for her. She complained: "We moved a mile across the corn fields and we lived there for eight years and it would have been from there to the cemetery. The plots were already purchased." Another woman found both the man and the house she had always dreamed of. At first, it seemed as if she would finally find happiness. She reports:

> My second husband had property in the mountains and that really appealed to me. I wanted to get away . . . So we started building a big house up on top of a mountain and, to me, that was like a bastion or something . . . I've been there for thirteen years . . . I felt like I couldn't devote myself to serious study, which is what I wanted to do. I felt very tied down because of where we lived. Every day I had to meet the school bus. It's not like being in a city where your child can walk home or walk to a day care center. It's the curse of the upper-middle class, the suburban things, you know.

Both of the above ended in divorce. Almost one-fifth of the women in this age group may find themselves facing a divorce (Cf. Rubin, 1979:27). For these people reengagement in the labor market may be imminent. They may be facing changes which they never thought possible.

Douglas Hall (1975) informs us that most women expect relief upon entering the Shrinking Circle Stage, but, in fact, the opposite seems to be true. The conflicts which began in the Peak Stage and the Full House Plateau may even increase.

Introduction to the Identity/Integrity Crisis

> I had the two real young and then it came to the age where they were getting ready to go to school and there weren't any decent jobs and I didn't know what to do with myself and I think I really consciously got pregnant the third time to fill in something . . . So I had three kids under the age of five and then they began growing up and my whole life was driving for Cub Scouts, driving for football, driving to the dentist, the orthodontist and taking lunches to the field . . . I began to feel totally powerless . . . I was a robot and I needed to fill in other people's lives but I had no life . . . Then it reached the point where my kids were eleven, twelve and thirteen and they had reached the age where they didn't need me . . . I was beginning to feel like a lot of my care for them was custodial, laundry type stuff . . . It was like I am this incredible unique woman and maybe 25 percent of me was being used in that situation. The whole rest of me that made me any different from any other woman nobody wanted . . . It was still untouched . . . My husband didn't know what to do with it and I verbalized that to him. I began to

get in touch with — Like you get married and you don't know what marriage is and so you accept whatever is going on because that's all you know of marriage and women don't talk about the heartaches. As I got older and read more and knew more people, what I got in touch with was what my marriage wasn't and what I felt were these holes, these huge black voids that I didn't know what should be there . . .

George Letchworth (1970) coined a term, "identity-integrity" to refer to a complex set of symptoms which he observed in his full-time homemaker clients at the University Counseling Center at Youngstown State University. The identity crisis, on the one hand, involves coming to terms with abilities and limitations, cultural values and attitudes, and with the means of occupying a suitable occupational societal role. Letchworth attributes recognition of this crisis to Erickson (1963). He states that women achieve some resolution of this crisis when they become wives and mothers, but that they often question their identities again after ten or fifteen years of marriage. The integrity crisis involves active participation in understanding the world from a "creative and unique perspective rather than from a conservative perspective."

Women caught in this identity/integrity crisis are reevaluating their lives for a variety of reasons. Among the most salient is boredom caused by children leaving the nest, perceiving their lives to be dull in comparison with their husbands', or lack of fulfillment from participation in women's organizations. Secondly, the desire to have an interesting job comes into play, which permits women to pursue personal interests while making an "active contribution" to the family. Escape from responsibilities may also be an issue, but, more importantly, divorce and marital difficulties may be major factors contributing to the crisis (Cf. Letchworth, 1970).

The women Letchworth is referring to are middle or upper middle class, as are the women in this study, and indeed, there are many overlaps between Letchworth's observations and the concerns alluded to by the women interviewed herein. People in the Shrinking Circle Stage mentioned an average of three main areas of pressure in their lives. In order of importance, the main problems emerged as follows:

1. Time
2. Children
3. Self/Home/School

Marriage conspicuously disappears from the list of pressures indicated by these women at this stage of life. This is interesting with regard to the fact that studies show that women are experiencing more negative perceptions of their marriages as they pass through each subsequent life stage. Mary Alice Beyer and Robert N. Whitehurst (1976) note that "something in marriage makes it more difficult for females in older age groups" and they claim that the reverse is true for men. The problem, they note, seems to be one of alienation. Yet Lillian Rubin (1979) finds that women "of a certain age" cling to their marriages and we have seen that the divorce rate for this age group is high.

Those who are divorced in this age group cease to mention the search for a partner as a concern and those who are married seem to accept their marriages as they are. This would seem to concur with Hall's (1975) findings which show home emerging as a dominant concern as women pass through the life stages. Home, however, is an overriding category within which women perceive many components.

Children were a concern second only to time, the perpetual problem for women. In this case, children and time are practically indivisible. Just when women are beginning to separate themselves somewhat from the family by pursuing external activities, children begin to demand time. All of the women entering the Shrinking Circle Stage still had children at home and many felt that these children resented any time that they spent away from the home. One stated: "I think they feel that I do a lot . . . I think that they only think in terms of time. How much time can I spend with them?" Another sees that:

> They don't like my being busy all the time. They tell me that I'm always busy and we don't have time to do the fun things that we used to and I tell them that it's temporary, that it won't always be like this, but I need their help.

Self, home and school take on equal weight for women in this cohort. Most of them are in the midst of a personal crisis, an identity/integrity crisis, which they hope to resolve by focusing on external activities such as school.

In the Shrinking Circle Stage, women are increasingly anticipating the "empty nest." They take on activities which they hope will provide stability through the coming life stages. Seventy-five percent of the women in the present study were trying to develop a new career to carry them through. In order to accomplish this goal, they had entered institutions of higher education. Perhaps this phenomenon could be called anticipatory socialization, preparing for changes which lie ahead.

Not only do women anticipate the empty nest, but they anticipate death of spouse at this stage.

> My mom didn't ever expect to be a widow. She had five children. Her plan was to have a huge family and be home. She was also planning to have a lot of money too. My father was a doctor so she figured, well, they'd have a big house and a large family and everything would be hunky dory but it didn't work out so I guess I have that realization that things don't always work out like you want them to and you could be forty-five or fifty and have to support yourself so I have to do something.

Another woman feared:

> If anything were to happen to my husband I'd be in big trouble because he is the sole support of the family and I have never had a career that would equal—you know—be able to keep up with the life style right now that he has done. My husband's father passed away five or six years ago and my mother-in-law had never worked. She had always devoted all to home and family and never really developed herself. She was happy doing that but now she is struggling financially and it hurts to see her have to do that. He died suddenly of a heart attack. You know you have to think about this.

This form of anticipatory socialization is not for nought. The age range of women in the Shrinking Circle Stage was forty-two to fifty-two, and again, they may have thirty more years to live. Most of them were married to men older than themselves, which is the norm in this country, with men being an average of three years older than their wives (Cf. Glick, 1976). In addition, since men die about seven years before women on the average, that leaves ten years of widowhood for women to consider.

Thus, boredom with life as it is, anticipation of children leaving home, and death of spouse are all part of the Identity/Integrity Crisis which seems to strike women at ever younger ages as the social conditons rapidly change. The contemporary American middle class family is dealing with new variables in the life cycle. The family is smaller, which implies that the period of family building will be shorter, the number and timing of the children's births are more likely to be planned to minimize negative effects on the mother's health, the degree of need for women to devote themselves full-time for many years to childbearing and childrearing is lessened and the couple can now provide more adequately for their growing children (Cf. Glick, 1976).

Probably the most dramatic change that has occurred as a result of these structural changes for the family is a much longer empty nest period. This effect has a multitude of social, psychological and economic ramifications.

The Minimal Circle Stage

The Minimal Circle Stage begins when all of the children have left home. For our sample, this stage began as young as age forty-three, with the average age of women interviewed in the Minimal Circle Stage falling in at fifty-three.

The allocation of time for these women, and the problems they mentioned in their lives, had changed very much from earlier stages. For example, the number of hours spent on housework for women in this stage was about twenty-nine, a difference of twelve hours a week in comparison with women in the Shrinking Circle Stage.

Women in the Minimal Circle Stage mentioned an average of one-and-a-half major pressure points in life. Money, not surprisingly, emerged as the number one concern. This was followed by time and school which carried equal weight. Money was of the greatest concern to the women who found themselves widowed and on fixed incomes. Their Identity/Integrity crises were often related to the death of a spouse and, for some, their imminent reengagements into the labor force came as a surprise. They sought to reengage through attaining more formal education, thus the concern with school. Reasons with the concern for time, or not having enough of it, are self-evident.

For most, husband and children had ceased to be great problems. The children were out on their own. The husbands were involved in their careers. This period was very difficult for women who had not engaged in the anticipatory socialization mentioned earlier in that they found themselves in the position of what Burgess called the "roleless role" which often comes with major role losses for older people (Cf. Atchley, 1972:156).

> My age has caused me to feel dissatisfied and unhappy. By age fifty you should have your life pretty well wrapped up and have your intermediate goals achieved. You should have your life wrapped

up to the point where you have a pretty clear picture of the future or something is very wrong.

Yet, as we have seen, women in previous history have not had such extended empty nest periods. Older women today have few role models for constructive approaches to this lengthy period of life. Many go into therapy to sort out their dilemmas.

> I had therapy. I was really concerned because I was drinking a lot and I was crying a lot. I was going through the – What is it, when the kids leave the nest? The Empty Nest Syndrome. [The kids] had been such a crusade for me. I felt like I was the only one who cared about them . . . So my crusade was gone . . . I was on pretty much of a destructive binge and the therapy was marvelous.

Answers to this problem are as varied and individual as each person who enters the Minimal Circle Stage. Some have worked it out long before they get there, as early as in the Peak Stage. Others wait until they suddenly find themselves in the quandary of the Minimal Circle. Regardless, most women must deal with the possibility of the "roleless role" unless they can come up with a scheme for thwarting it. Many women are turning to higher education for answers.

Marriage, the birth of children, children leaving home, the "empty nest" and widowhood are all major turning points in women's adult lives. They merit much study, particularly in light of the fact that women's work in the labor force, in general, depends on the stage of their family and other family factors.

In the next chapter, we will take a closer look at the meaning of children in the adult life cycle.

4
The Motherhood Mandate: Part of a Package Deal

Is Biology Destiny?

Reentry women perceive few choices at the time of marriage. Career is not an issue for the overwhelming majority. They feel that being the nurturant partner in marriage and the socializing agent of the children will be fulfilling work. Nonetheless, as we shall see later, many of them begin to feel isolated, removed from public life, "prisoners" of the "upper middle class dream." Why are they so enamored, at first, of this particular destiny?

For the moment, at least, let us assume that biology is destiny. Let us assume, as many investigators have in the past, that women's biological function (maternity and motherhood) outweighs their motivation to achieve. The argument, as Juliet Mitchell (1973) has so wryly noted, runs as follows:

> The biological function of maternity is a universal, atemporal fact . . . From it is made to follow the so-called stability and omnipresence of the family . . . Once this is accepted, women's social

57

subordination – however emphasized as an honorable, but different role (cf. the equal-but-"separate" ideologies of Southern racists) – can be seen to follow inevitably as an *insurmountable* bio-historical fact. The causal chain goes: maternity, family, absence from production and public life, sexual inequality.

But can this biological function alone be enough to explain women's absence from public life and production? More explicitly, can the idea that biology equals destiny explain women's absence from powerful positions in public life? It may be that motherhood alone is the culprit.

Jessie Bernard in *The Future of Motherhood* (1974) claims that many women are actually "coerced" into becoming mothers. She states that we emphasize the importance of motherhood to women and thus foreclose alternative roles to them. How do we do this? We teach girls to be feminine "so that they will not only opt for motherhood but will feel satisfied with it and even fight any change that may threaten it." (1974:25) This is done by processing women to want children and it is accomplished through parents, schools, churches, laws, the media and governmental policy.

Girls are processed into the mother role from the time they are born. Little girls aspire to be mothers whereas little boys aspire to be firemen, aviators, and astronauts (Bernard, 1974). Girls are further encouraged by school books wherein sex-typed models are presented. Bernard refers to these images as the child's "first encounters with her own future" (p. 26). There is small doubt that the little girl will become a mother. Voluntary childlessness is still considered deviant behavior, and only a small percentage of women can expect not to bear children (Cf. Veevers, 1972).

Finally, religion and art have glorified the image of the mother. The use of toys, images in story books, television serials, commercials and daytime soap operas, games and school patterns have all abetted girls' desires to become mothers. Public opinion and subsidies have encouraged motherhood and laws against contraception, abortion and infanticide have provided negative sanctions (Cf. Bernard, 1974:28).

Maternity and family have caused, for women, higher absentee rates on the job (someone must care for sick children) and higher turnover rates. Women have taken jobs which they can easily move in and out of with fluctuations in their family responsibilities. The argument Juliet Mitchell cites is perpetuated.

Adrienne Rich, author of *Of Woman Born* (1976) shares some of her own perceptions of motherhood:

> I did not understand that this circle, this magnetic field [of mother and children] in which we lived, was not a natural phenomenon . . . the emotion-charged, tradition-heavy form in which I found myself cast as the Mother seemed . . . as ineluctable as the tides, (p. 4).

There were times when she felt the pressure of motherhood so greatly that she believed only death might free her from her children, times when she "envied the barren woman who has the luxury of her regrets but lives a life of privacy and freedom" (Cf. Rich, 1976:1). It only occurred to her much later in life that she might examine that word 'barren" in a less emotional, more rational sense which might illuminate some of the assumptions she carried with her as standard baggage upon her entry into adulthood, upon "becoming a wife."

It has only been in very recent years that women have begun to examine the characteristics and components of motherhood in America and the implications for women of becoming mothers, particularly in terms of stratification and power differentials in society. Most find that there is an overwhelming mandate in the United States for women to become mothers regardless of trends in technology which alleviate the inevitability of motherhood and alter women's roles in the labor force. It has been a common notion that women must become mothers or remain forever unfulfilled as women (Cf. Bernard, 1974).

The Question of Nonmotherhood

As we have already seen, only about 10 percent of women at any given time remain childless (Cf. Glick, 1976). This figure includes single as well as married women. Because 90 percent of women will become mothers, women tend to take motherhood for granted. But, what of those who do not, that four or so percent who do not desire children?

Women who do not desire to have children or who are incapable of bearing children may face severe social sanctions. As previously mentioned, they continue to be regarded as rare and deviant. Only since the late 1960s has motherhood become a political issue wherein people are questioning the birthrate in the United States (Cf. Bernard, 1974:268). This is due to a complex melding of ecological, economic and environmental issues.

A study of reference group support for voluntary childlessness found that women who chose to remain childless found reference groups to support that decision, yet they had fewer reference groups than women who wanted children. Both groups were very much aware of social pressures and sanctions which coerce women into having babies but those who did not desire children showed less concern about these sanctions (Cf. Houseknecht, 1977). The study concluded that both sets of women conformed to the social norms of groups within which they were operating.

What are these reference groups that encourage women to remain "childfree?" In a book entitled *A Baby . . . Maybe,* Elizabeth Whelan (1975) discusses contemporary reference groups on both sides of the issue. The antinatalist groups, organizations which strive to reduce the birth rate, include Zero Population Growth (ZPG) and the National Organization for Non-Parents (NON). They attack "media pressure" which encourages women to become mothers.

> For instance, ZPG members are upset because an Ivory Snow television advertisement features mom, two boys, and an infant. Three children! They are concerned about the Mary Worth Cartoon strip because its creators let a rather liberated female character submit to her husband's unreasonable demand that she quit her job and play housewife and mother. And they are furious with the *National Enquirer* for sponsoring a search for America's oldest father with a child under twelve months of age. (Whelan, 1975:36).

Antinatalist groups are relatively new on the social scene. Pronatalist groups, encouraging birth, have been around for centuries. Arguing this side of the issue are religious leaders, family traditionalists, most of one's friends and neighbors and even insurance salesmen (Cf. Whelan, 1975:22). Potential grandmothers are an effective pronatalist pressure group. J. E. Veevers (1973) finds that negative sanctions directed at childless couples are most intense during the fourth and fifth years of marriage. All of the childless wives interviewed in Veevers' study felt that they were to some extent stigmatized by their decision not to have children, or, more explicitly, to avoid having children until such time as all desire for having children had passed. They felt they could be categorized by a "ubiquitous negative stereotype" which includes such attributions as abnormality, selfishness, immorality, irresponsibility, immaturity, unhappiness, unfulfillment and nonfeminine behavior. In addition, they felt that, while people never seem to have to account for why they chose to have children, they often had to account for why they chose not to. In other words, in order to remain childless, they had to develop ideologies which would allow them to do so without guilt. Generally, childless women tend to develop defense mechanisms to enhance their positions. These include

1. Selective perception of the consequences of motherhood;
2. Differential association resulting in physical and psychological isolation from conflicting world views;
3. Structuring trial motherhood so as to reaffirm existing biases, and;
4. Capitalizing upon contemporary social ambivalence toward parenthood. (Cf. Veevers, 1975).

As Veevers states, this adds up to a process for accounting for childlessness that may be exceedingly difficult.

In some studies, an inverse relationship has been found between amount of education and number of births. The higher a woman's education, the fewer children she will have. This only seems to apply, however, to women under thirty years of age. It makes no difference in those over thirty (Cf. Ritchey and Stokes, 1974). Perhaps this can be attributed to the recency of emergence of the antinatalist support and reference groups.

Finally, it appears that even childless women perceive children to be an essential component of marriage. R. M. Kierfert and G. I. J. Dixon (1968) discovered that childless women and women with children agreed in the following areas:

1. The belief that childless women should attempt to have children;
2. The belief that childless women desire children;
3. The belief that childless women envy women with children;
4. The belief that women with children do not envy childless females.

Further, it was noted that husbands' attitudes were very significant in the decision to remain childless. About one-third of the childless husbands, but only 7 percent of the childless wives, stated that they did not want children. One-third of the childless people felt guilty about their childless condition.

Thus, for women, whether or not to become mothers is not a question generally asked. Motherhood has accompanied wifehood and vice versa. The women in our study had little or no support from antinatalist groups and they were bombarded with pronatalist propaganda from all sides. All but one quickly and quietly succumbed to the motherhood role. Some were thrilled and others detested the prospect.

Planning and Fatalism:
Approaches to Motherhood

Let us digress for a moment to the one woman included in the study who was not a mother. Why was she included in a study which called for women who "have been raising children and are now coming back to school?" The answer is simple. The time in her adult life since Becoming a Wife had been oriented around her husband and would have been oriented around children, but, she never carried a baby to term. It was only after some years went by that she and her husband came to the realization that neither of them had really wanted children anyway. She was the only woman interviewed who found herself faced with a real choice, and it was not by choice, initially, that she did not become a mother. She told her story this way:

> I was never crazy about kids. I came from a large family. I always had to babysit. I never had any free time . . . I was never really crazy about kids but I always felt that when you get married, you should have kids, you know, but not more than two and when we got married, people always told my husband what a good father he would make so I said, well, should we have kids or not? And, of course, I was twenty-nine years old at the time and I told him, "If I don't have any kids by the time I'm thirty, I'm not having any kids." So that first year we tried like hell because that was it . . . When nothing happened, I was under the impression that he wanted kids and he was disappointed. So, then after that year went by and I had had a miscarriage, we talked about it. He thought I wanted kids and I thought he did. We thought about adopting a kid. I wanted to talk it out completely, make it perfectly clear, because I didn't want him to say later that I was the ogre or something and he said, "No, Jane, I don't want any kids," and I said, "Oh, God, am I glad you said that because I don't really want any either."

This couple had reached a happy agreement in the end. The cost, however, had been a period of uncomfortable ambivalence in their marriage. Still,

Jane volunteered to participate in this study and considered herself a "reentry woman who had been spending the previous years with her family and was now coming back in."

Most of the forty-four mothers interviewed in this study felt, as Jane did, that "when you get married, you should have kids." Most saw children as inevitable and a logical extension of the marriage.

Discussing Children   The women were asked, "When did you and your husband seriously think about having children?" Categories provided for answers included the following: Before Marriage, During the First Year of Marriage, Never Thought About It, and, Other (Specify). Twenty-nine out of forty-five women could not classify their response according to these categories and opted for Other. For all twenty-nine, it was assumed that they would become mothers. They did not discuss it with their husbands with the exception of the occasional discussion about the whens and wherefores of parenting. No discussions were held on the ifs. One woman stated: "We talked about children as something in the foreseeable future . . . Children went with the romantic view of marriage."

And another felt that having children

> . . . was sort of assumed at that time. It was simply a financial question too because it would take a few years for us to have enough money. We did talk about it as though it was a choice but I don't think it was really a choice.

The only choices involved had to do with timing. Five women said they had felt that the first baby would come when their husbands finished school. One had felt that they would have a baby when her husband got a good job. Thus they wanted to be in good financial positions to support children and they did not wish to have to work to help support the family. Very few women discussed the prospect of children with their husbands before marriage.

As we saw in chapter 3, most of these women had had their first baby by the time they were twenty-three-and-one-half years old. By age twenty-eight, they had completed their childbearing. In some cases, planning was involved, but this was unusual. Women tended to enter into motherhood unaware, not knowing what to expect and with little support once they became pregnant. Many were unprepared to meet the demands of the job. If they worked toward children in a financial

or educational sense, they did not often work toward children in a psychological sense.

> I got pregnant. It was planned but I didn't think I'd get pregnant
> that quickly. Then we had a baby . . . I stopped working and became
> a mother. That was probably the worst adjustment I've ever made
> because things were different then. There was no support. It was the
> Dark Ages. This is really emotional to me. It was the worst time
> in my life and also I had the worst baby you could have, the most
> difficult to take care of. She cried all the time. She was always
> awake. She didn't eat well. She didn't sleep well. She didn't like
> strangers so I couldn't leave her with babysitters. It was a particu-
> larly difficult situation. I was totally unprepared. And it was not
> acceptable for a mother to have an outside commitment and that
> was wrong for me. I had gone from having gone to school and
> working full-time to being in this little apartment with this scream-
> ing baby. It was horrible. I went to a physical fitness class at the
> Y when the baby was about four months old because they provided
> babysitting. That was the key. That was something. I went to a
> shrink when she was about six months old but he was a male chau-
> vinist shrink and that just made things worse. I still feel upset when
> I think about it. He didn't say too much but when I talked about
> going back to work or back to school, I'd get all these negative
> vibrations. A mother shouldn't be thinking about those things,
> so he just made it worse.

Although it was not part of the interview, at least 25 percent of the
women mentioned were seeing psychiatrists, psychologists or counselors
to discuss problems which arose in connection with marriage and motherhood. In other words, planning whether or not to have children, per se,
was not an option, even when women were unprepared or did not feel
like "natural born mothers." Planning the number and spacing of children, however, was seen as a viable choice. These were decisions wherein
the women could take an active role in determining their personal futures
and the futures of their families as well.

Planning the Number and Spacing of Children   Fifty-five percent of the
women planned the number of children that they ultimately had. They
desired between one and five children. The majority wanted two. Half
of the mothers also planned the spacing of their children. Thirty-nine
percent did not plan the number, however, and 36 percent did not plan
the spacing. This means that about half of the women were planners,

about a third did not plan and the rest varied from those who tried and failed, those who could not remember and those who never gave it a thought one way or the other.

In response to the question, "Would you say that generally speaking you planned for the future or did you take each day as it came during your early marriage and childbearing years?" over two-thirds of the women interviewed claimed to have taken each day as it came. Three women said they planned for their husbands' futures, but that their own futures were never considered. Eight women said that they had tried to plan for the future. Most of them differentiated between planning for the future and planning the number and spacing of their children's births. This is interesting in light of the fact that mothering comprised their major adult role during these years. Nonetheless, they found it difficult to plan under the circumstances of changing geographical locations and precarious or non-existent positions in the labor force. They were often ambivalent or resentful about answering this question. One woman complained:

> Planned for my future or planned for our future together in the marriage? Planning for my future, no, I did not. I thought I was planning for my future by planning a future together in the marriage, but when it came down to it, my future and *the* future could not cohabitate.

When Audrey Chamberlain (1976) asked a group of women with many children, "Would you say that generally speaking you planned for the future, or do you take each day as it comes?", well over half of the respondents said that they took each day as it came. Only nine women, out of her sample of 100, said that they planned. The planning that they did was of limited scope. They planned holidays and they saved money to buy clothes, for example. The nonplanning mothers claimed that they could not plan because there was not enough money, the future was too uncertain, their plans often did not work out or they felt their husband's work situation was insecure. Chamberlain concluded that unplanned pregnancies were part of a total fatalistic outlook concerning the future and toward pregnancy in general. For most of the mothers she studied, planning was a desirable approach to life but it seemed unobtainable. The women in Chamberlain's study felt that trying to plan was irrational in light of their situation, and that to plan would be to "court disappointment." The women in the present study also held a rather fatalistic orientation to life in general, specifically with respect to planning. Though they had planned for the future of the family, they had been fatalistic about their own futures during their early marriage and childbearing years.

Luck, Fate and the Probability of Conception   Audrey Chamberlain also discovered that mothers felt that the size of their families was something over which they had little or no control. In answer to the question, "What part would you say luck/fate plays in how many children you have?", some women reported they believed that the number of births occurring to a given woman was a matter fated for her, some believing in predestination, some called it bad luck and some felt that certain women conceived more easily than others. Almost two-thirds of the women she interviewed said that fate played a large part in the number of children they were to have.

Fifty-six percent (n=25) of the women we interviewed felt that luck or fate played a part in the number of children they had. Thirty-six percent (n=16) felt that luck or fate played no part. All of those claiming the irrelevance of luck or fate in determining family size believed strongly in birth control methods and in the high reliability of these measures when used properly. The women who felt that luck or fate played a role gave the following predominant reasons:

1. Reproduction cannot be perfectly regulated even with birth control;
2. Divorce intercedes when women might want to have more children;
3. Some women have a hard time getting pregnant;
4. Twins are sometimes a surprise;
5. Money and relationships with husbands play a role;
6. Religion can play a strong role;
7. Ultimately, one's fate is in the hands of God.

Women do not have to be "high fertility" mothers, as those in Chamberlain's sample were, to feel that the number of children they will bear is somewhat dependent on luck or fate. One woman commented:

> I don't know. I would either say it was luck or fate or both . . . I certainly didn't plan on having the fourth child at all . . . You could say it was luck or you could say it was unlucky.

Regardless of the fact that most of the women believed in luck or fate, forty-four out of forty-five women believed in, and approved of, birth control measures. Most of them strongly approved and used contraceptive pills or devices. The one woman who did not approve of birth control cited her religious convictions as the reason. The women tried to control their pregnancies, but it did not work out the way they had planned in many cases.

Nearly half of the women interviewed experienced unwanted pregnancies. This factor alone made it difficult for these women to chart a course with specific goals for their adult lives. When asked, "How many times did you become pregnant that you wished you hadn't?", twenty women out of forty-five (45 percent) answered that this had happened at least once. For ten women, unwanted pregnancies occurred more than once. The number of unwanted pregnancies per person ranged from one to five. In all, thirty-seven unwanted pregnancies were reported. Despite legal prohibitions and stigma, four of these pregnancies terminated in abortion. Three unwanted pregnancies terminated in miscarriages to the relief of the mothers and one unwanted pregnancy ended in putting the child out for adoption.

In sum, eight of the unwanted pregnancies did not result in the mother's taking on another child to raise. What of the remaining twenty-five? Twenty-five initially unwanted children were borne and raised and nurtured by sixteen self-sacrificing mothers. These mothers relinquished personal goals and freedom of choice for children they reared and, most often, to whom they dedicated their lives.

Many felt that the kids "had been such a crusade for me. I felt like I was the only one who cared about them." Most accepted these children and came to terms with the "inevitability" of motherhood during pregnancy. The women felt it was their "lot" to be mothers.

Worry Over Pregnancy Of the women experiencing unwanted pregnancies, fourteen had experienced mild to intense worry over becoming pregnant. Two-thirds of the entire sample feared pregnancy, particularly during marriage. In fact, the large majority of unwanted pregnancies had occurred during the "safety" of wedlock. Only six people who experienced unwanted pregnancies had never worried about the prospect. They were, in general, ambiguous about their adult roles as women and mothers. They found motherhood more demanding than they had imagined. There were trials and tribulations that they had not counted on.

Most of the women had expressed the desire to have children in the beginning of married life. Only one woman stated that she really wanted no children, yet she ended up with five unwanted pregnancies and three children.

Worry over pregnancy increased with each passing year of married life. Each subsequent child was more difficult when added to the total number of responsibilities the woman had incurred. Though many started out wanting four or more children, they found that two children pushed them to the limit of their resources. If a woman had already borne two or three children, she often saw additional pregnancies as extremely traumatic, particularly if she viewed her family as complete. One woman describes her experience this way:

> I had four children close together, then ten years later, I had another one ... Along about 1967 I really got the urge to go back [to work] and I communicated with the State Department of Education to find out what it would take to renew my teaching certificate and before I even began to take the courses I would need, I was pregnant. I knew I was pregnant and so I just dropped everything ... It was a shock the fifth time I got pregnant. It was stronger than surprise. It was shock.

Diane Vinokur-Kaplan (1977) found by questioning 141 white American couples that having over two children strains the family's resources in the areas of time, energy and commitments. Areas of concern reported by parents included altruism (giving oneself to children), the workload of the spouse, time for self and with spouse, economic needs and the concern for the emotional and social needs of children. Particularly, concerns for one's own time, work and interests deterred the respondents from wanting the additional children. Certainly this was a consideration of the women interviewed herein.

Hindsight: Choices They might Have Made

Fewer than one-third of the women were happy with the ultimate outcome of their families with regard to family size. The remainder did not end up with what they perceived as the ideal number of children. A few wished they had had more children but the great majority wished that they had fewer (see Table 4.1).

Five women wished that they might have had one more child. Unfortunately, luck or fate, in the form of divorce or physical problems, had intervened. Most often, these were women with only one child.

One-third of the women interviewed, fifteen women, wished that they would not have had so many children. They claimed to "love their children," but expressed some regret in that "life might have been different." With hindsight, ambivalent feelings were common:

> If you have children at all . . . Well, I have mixed emotions about this. I don't know how I would feel if I didn't have children, if I would feel differently . . . As of now, I need at least the one I've got. I don't want any more. At the maximum, one child is the ideal number.

Why do you consider this number ideal?

> I just don't have the patience for more than one. I thought I liked kids. I really don't, you know. Until my daughter was ten, she couldn't even have kids in the house because they drive me crazy. They break things. One's sufficient to do all the mothering you need to do.

Four women felt that "one is sufficient." One would have allowed them to mother, to fulfill their desires to "do the mother kinds of things."

> One would have been sufficient for me, for myself. In retrospect, well, knowing that – Not having a sense of aloneness, knowing that something belongs to me and I belong to someone. That's not really true, but it's a sense of belonging.

This woman had three children. Women who had more children than they wished felt that luck or fate had definitely played a role. Some saw it as an "act of God." Yet they concurred that they loved their children and were accepting of them even when they were not planned.

In fact, all but six women still would have had children if they had it to do over. Mothering was that important. It filled a need. It created an adult role. These six women had serious misgivings about having had any children at all. Some felt like this woman:

> I wanted four children in the beginning. Ideal for me now? . . . I can't really say. I have found I am not the mother type I once was forcing myself to be but at the same time I love all my children.

Another expressed a similar conflict:

> I don't know whether I would have children [if I had it to do over]. I have very mixed feelings about it. I've sort of been left holding the bag. My ideal was four and now, I just don't know.

"Now, I just don't know." One of the causes of this ambivalence may be trends in fashion.

TABLE 4.1

PRIOR IDEAL, ACTUAL AND RETROSPECTIVE IDEAL FAMILY SIZE

*Considerations Concerning
Family Size*

Number of Children	Desired Family Size Prior to Marriage	Achieved Family Size	Retrospective Ideal Family Size
0	1 (2%)		6 (14%)
1–2	12 (27%)	28 (64%)	29 (66%)
3–4	13 (30%)	14 (32%)	8 (18%)
5–6	6 (14%)	2 (5%)	1 (2%)
7+	3 (7%)	0	0
Never Thought About It	9 (20%)	0	0
Total No. of Women	44 (100%)	44 (100%)	44 (100%)

Ideal Family Size: Trends in Fashion?

Jessie Bernard states: "It may seem bizarre to view as a matter of fashion anything so fundamental as ideal family size. But so it seems to be" (1974:57). In general, the number of children that people consider to be ideal is larger than the number of children they expect to have. Bernard (1974) notes that in 1966 a summary of thirteen studies dealing with ideal family size concluded that the ideal family size perceived remained fairly constant, fluctuating between two and four. Prior to the 1950s, two seemed the ideal number. This increased to four in the 1950s and currently the trend is back down to two. What factors contribute to these changes in desired family size?

One emergent phenomenon is the fact that women are entering the labor force in ever greater numbers. This is due to economic necessity and the rising aspirations of American women. John Scanzoni (1976) found that women who are more highly educated are more likely to be egalitarian in their perception of gender role norms and they may delay their entry into marriage, "biding their time until they can strike an equitable arrangement regarding reciprocal rights and duties." Thus, perceptions of sex role norms indirectly affects fertility through the timing of marriage. The more highly educated women are, the more time they expect to spend in the labor force and the fewer children they expect to have. More specifically, the more gratified women are with paid work, the less motivated they are to have large numbers of children (Cf. Scanzoni, 1976).

Jerome Schmelz (1976) reports similar findings. He demonstrates an inverse relationship between the percentages of women entering the labor force and the birth rate in the 1960s. He claims that "women today expect more out of their adult lives than being just mothers and homemakers which has meant a growing expectation that they will work outside the home." In order to support his hypothesis he presented the following explanations:

1. The re-emergence of the women's liberation movement which he sees as the "barometer" of women's rising aspirations and discontent with the traditional female roles of housewifery and motherhood;
2. The declining marriage rate among younger age groups;
3. The increased pursuit of higher education by women;
4. The increased female labor force participation rate;
5. The increased divorce rate.

Schmelz notes, in his argument, that rising occupational aspirations probably are most characteristic of college educated women.

In building an economic theory of fertility behavior, Robert Willis (1973) also cites wives' labor force participaton as a deterrent to large families. He weighs the economic costs and benefits of having children. Willis discusses the costs of children in terms of time, money, consumption, saving and investment considerations, problems with imperfect fertility control and age at marriage.

In general, the number of children considered to be ideal by the women in this sample was smaller than the number they actually had, a finding which is at odds with Bernard's (1974) conclusions concerning ideal family size. Why?

Perhaps it is the case that, for these women, with increasing aspirations, the value of children is lowered. This might be attributed to all of the factors listed above. Further, it would be plausible to attribute this to changes in the fashions of women's roles.

Fashion and the Value of Children

Scanzoni (1976), Schmelz (1976) and Willis (1973) all address the question, whether indirectly or overtly, of women's changing gender roles and fertility pattens. A study which directly measured conjugal role definitions and the value of children (Cf. Tobin, 1976) hypothesized that fertility differentials are a function of female role definitions assuming that a variety of marital roles are available. More specifically the hypothesis stated that the more domestic the conjugal role definition, the more beneficial the perceived consequences of children would be. After interviewing 433 married women, it was concluded that there was much doubt as to whether increased variation in conjugal roles will have any immediate effect on the family planning habits of women or their views toward children. This research shows that role definitions seem to bear little relationship to attitude toward children in moderate education and income families.

Another investigator claims that it is a matter of the changing value of human time. As the value of human time rises, fertility will fall (Cf. Sawhill, 1977).

All in all, research results are ambiguous. Different investigators postulate different relationships among the birth rate, women's conjugal roles, the economic situation in the country and even fads in childbearing practices.

Only one fact remains constant: It is the rare woman indeed who does not become a mother and motherhood often creates barriers to women's full and equal participation in society outside of the family. These barriers are increasingly coming to be viewed as a social problem.

Mothers in the Work Force

Women's participation in the labor force has more than doubled since 1950. On the surface, it would seem that women are gaining more independence, but this is doubtful in light of the positions working women occupy, particularly when equated with their reasons for pursuing paid work.

The myth that women work to attain a little spending money has been largely dispelled at this point. The fact that women with children are entering the labor force at a faster rate than women without children (Cf. Bell, 1973) is probably a good indicator of the current economic position of the American family. Thirteen million working women in this country are heads of households themselves. In March 1972, these households included ten million children under the age of eighteen and reported a median income of $4,456 as compared to the median income of $11,810 for families composed of two parents and children (Cf. Bell, 1973). Nearly one-third of the women in the present sample were single heads of households at the time they were interviewed and many more of them had, at various times, been single heads of households. They, like millions of other women, were directing their efforts toward finding work because they had to.

Middle class women often seek other rewards from their work as well. They seek a sense of self-satisfaction and recognition for a job well done: benefits which accompany membership in the career-oriented work force. Although few women define work as a career that takes precedence over family duties in importance, work is becoming increasingly important particularly because women have more uninterrupted time in the adult life cycle in which to pursue it.

Unfortunately, though women are entering the labor force in greater and greater numbers, most of them hold jobs on the less prestigious rungs of the labor ladder. The women we interviewed were often clerical workers, a fact which holds true for women across the country. Women comprise approximately 80 percent of all clerical workers. When women become professionals, they are segregated into the lower rungs of professionalism.

Some of the problems that arise include the following:

1. Women are in the labor force, yet still taking care of most of the housework that is done in the home thus winding up with two "jobs";
2. Work and family roles are largely incompatible for women because of the inflexibility of the rules of the workplace;
3. Only enough daycare exists for about 10 percent of the children of working mothers;
4. The labor force tends to be sex-segregated;
5. There is a nonprovision of training for women in the labor force because employers do not want to invest in on-the-job training for females. Women have a higher rate of absenteeism and

voluntary turnover than men and they enter into jobs where extensive training is not required;

6. In addition to all of the above factors, motherhood is still "mandated" and sex role socialization leads women into motherhood (Cf. Zellman, 1976).

The result of all this is that when mothers work, they end up in low paying, sex-segregated jobs that require little on-the-job training and which are easy to move in and out of (Cf. Zellman, 1976).

Nonetheless, women must work and they must become mothers. As Jessie Bernard (1974) inquires, what do we want women to do?

Role Conflict in the Expanding Circle Stage

It has been noted that there is relatively little conflict concerning the roles of worker and mother for college students. Idealistically, college students assume that they will combine the roles of mother and paid worker in the "double track" pattern and attain fulfillment from each position.

However, when women are directly involved in mothering, they find time for little else. Even if they feel they have the ability to pursue two primary courses of activity, they may experience difficulty in obtaining daycare. If they do find help with childcare, they may be called frivolous, uncaring or immature as a consequence of leaving their children to be "raised by strangers." It often seems like a no-win situation.

It is likely that as women perceive the complexity of the motherhood experience firsthand, they realize that they are getting more (or less) than they bargained for. We have seen that two-thirds of the present sample ended up ambivalent about choices they had made concerning motherhood during early adulthood. They felt they had been unprepared for the extensive commitment which motherhood entails yet they were uncertain about other paths they might have chosen. The messages were mixed and role models experiencing no ambivalence were scarce.

They saw respected women such as Margaret Mead or Phyllis Chesler experiencing their own kinds of conflicts as they strove to combine motherhood with a successful career. And those women were well established before they even thought about children. Where does that leave the average woman?

Conflicted. It leaves most women conflicted. There are three main reasons for this.

First, more than two-thirds of the women we interviewed had been to college before marriage. They felt they possessed a strong individual potential which would "distinguish" them from other mothers. They felt that they could "do something more." They wanted to explore this, develop it and strive to make individual contributions to society.

Second, they saw their roles as "custodial" mother and primary care-taker of the children as temporally limited. By the time they were forty-five, most of the children would have left home. If they lived an average life, they would still have thirty years after the children were gone. By and large, they found themselves unprepared for this additional, albeit lengthy, segment of life and successful mentors were hardly abundant.

Third, a large number of women found themselves divorced or widowed, single heads of households, and forced to earn a living to sup-port children financially. As the years passed, women realistically antici-pated divorce or widowhood and they wondered why they had not been prepared for these dilemmas earlier in life. They realized they may be forced to earn a wage and that they were unprepared, untrained, unskilled and often considered undesirable by employers because of age and family commitments.

Though this quandary exists in no uncertain terms, and women feel it acutely, they still perceive little choice about having children. If they have any control at all, it is only with regard to how many children they will bear and how far apart they will be.

It seems that women often do not possess the resources and expecta-tions which they need in order to make decisions concerning their own future achievements. Planning anything other than the number and spacing of children is perceived as risky, setting oneself up for failure.

Essentially, future orientation does not exist until women are forced to make their own ways in the paid labor market or until they are spending so little time on childcare that they feel compelled to search for alternative involvements to fill the spaces in mid- and late-adulthood. In order to plan, mothers must perceive they have:

1. Adequate resources;
2. A faith in the reasonableness of what can be achieved or expected;
3. A desire for the "pay-off" or being able to think through the "opportunity-costs" available (Cf. Chamberlain, 1976).

Most of the time, as we shall see in the next chapter, these conditions exist only when mothers are facing a crisis situation. It is only in crisis that these women look toward the future.

The Question of Biology and Destiny Revisited

Occasionally when women begin to orient themselves toward the future, biology intercedes. The women we interviewed incurred a very high number of unwanted pregnancies, each of which contained the elements of a crisis within it. Fully one quarter of the children borne and reared by these women were initially unwanted. They were what we commonly term "accidents."

It would be highly unfair and simplistic to attribute these pregnancies to some deep-seated psychological desire. First of all, the phenomenon of unwanted pregnancy was more the rule than the exception. Secondly, these are hard-working women of dignity, integrity and responsibility.

Rather, birth control measures may not be as reliable as we believe. The reader may optimistically note that many of these children were born before technology made "birth control pills" so widely available. Yet, after a surge of usage of the "pill" in the 1960s and 1970s, so many negative side effects were discovered that women began to turn to "less reliable" birth control methods such as those used in the 1940s and 1950s. Perhaps technology has not freed women to the extent that we like to believe.

Biology still continues to interfere with the pursuit of excellence outside of marriage and family for women. Biology still is linked inextricably with the destiny of women.

5
Making the Transition

Upon marrying, many women drastically alter their involvements and activities. They stop working, they start working, they drop out of school, they move away from family and friends.

The great majority of the women interviewed had their first baby within the first two years of marriage. They were fully committed to their marital roles of wife- and motherhood. This demanded a certain attitude on their part.

Women were willing to work when it was necessary in order to maintain the family's standard of living. They were also willing to work to put their husbands through school but they did not consider earning an income to be a component of their role in marriage. That was primarily the husband's realm although they pitched in and helped whenever this action was called for. As a result they moved in and out of the labor force, primarily working in clerical jobs, organizing their work schedules around the demands of their husbands' jobs.

Though they did not expect to support their husbands financially, they did expect to provide the primary emotional support in the family. This component of the housewife role was viewed as paramount by most women. They would do "whatever was necessary" to insure that their husbands could move ahead in jobs or careers. This often meant relocating at various intervals to follow the job market.

Even though the moves left women feeling uprooted and lonely, they still felt that it was their "duty" to comply. As many mentioned, whatever enhanced their husband's career also enhanced their own standard of living and contributed positively to their children's opportunities.

As a result of the wifely role they had incurred in marriage, it would have been unrealistic for these women to consider possibilities for their own futures apart from their marital relationships or apart from their roles as mothers. They felt that it was their responsibility to assume the role of the primary child rearer.

During the early years of the marriage, it had been important for them as individuals to focus on their internal, within the home, involvements, particularly when it came to raising children. That was the job of a mother. Without questioning, they had moved into the routines which they had been socialized to expect upon becoming adults.

Because the routines had been prescribed in advance, the women entered into marriage somewhat cognizant of what their roles would entail. Their husbands also expected a specific type of involvement which they were clear about. They would primarily be the breadwinners, the providers.

So, a status quo was established in the family system. Tasks were clearly divided and it was in this sense that the marriages and the families of these women attained a specific equilibrium and established a specific division of labor.

For the forty hours a week that husbands spent working in the labor force, the wives spent at least forty hours a week working in the household. We have seen that they cooked, sewed, canned, gardened, decorated and redecorated, stimulated and encouraged their children and acted as sounding board and cheering section for their husbands.

The women's lives revolved around their families and the major commitment was to the success of their families as entities. This demanded flexibility.

The Contingency Orientation as a Mechanism for Coping with the Housewife Routine

Flexibility and adaptability became the bywords of this era. Women congratulated themselves on their abilities to contend with sudden changes. They accomplished this adaptibility by being highly geographically mobile, by being transitionally unemployed and by being oriented to the present rather than to the future, taking each day as it came. They made few demands concerning their own futures apart from the marriage and family situation and, in most cases, it did not even occur to them to do so.

Shirley Angrist and Elizabeth Almquist (1975) have identified this behavior in college women. They coined the term "contingency orientation" to explain it. In other words, any plans which women may have with regard to engaging in activities external to the family are contingent upon the stage of the family and their roles within the family system. Angrist and Almquist deem this approach as "open" and they refer to it in the following manner:

> They [college women] do not peg their plans on a single hook; instead they expect, realistically, to incorporate a number of roles into their adult lives. Such openness helps them cope with the many demands on their lives – marriage, child-rearing, work, community involvement, and the myriad of other activities they expect to have (p. 32-33).

But even more to the point, the contingency orientation is the "If Syndrome." *If* we live near the YWCA, then I will take up dancing. *If* my daughter can go to nursery school, then I may get a job in a department store. *If* my husband gets transferred to Ohio, then I may take up embroidery on a serious basis.

The contingency orientation acts as a coping mechanism when wives and mothers become uprooted through relocation, for example. This mental framework can come to form the basis for women's attitudes with respect to their personal goals. They must hold a contingency orientation toward external involvements if they expect their family to remain a cohesive unit. Someone must compromise and they perceive this "other orientation" as a major component of the wife/mother role complex.

Many women, however, view the contingency orientation as a temporary outlook. Some women become disenchanted with this outlook early on in marriage and are divorced. Others foresee an end to their total other orientation as children leave the nest. Most people begin to anticipate closure with regard to this particular orientation when the last child is born. At this time they begin to anticipate the eventual termination of the maternal aspects of their adult lives.

Though many women adopt this contingency orientation, we cannot assume that it is what they desire. The women in our sample often grew weary of their "one day at a time" outlooks. They could not set long range goals for themselves outside of the family situation.

The idea of moving in and out of the labor force because of family needs grew less and less attractive. Some women tired of moving around the United States, continually leaving friends, family and social identities behind. Others began to feel powerless, out of control of their own futures. They began to reevaluate their lives, their philosophies and their identities.

Arriving at a Transition

All of the women in this study were passing through a transitional period. For some, the motivation to change the structure of their lives came from deep within themselves. They sought higher achievements unrelated to marriage. They sought external involvement as a matter of self-fulfillment. For others, the motivation for change was the result of an unanticipated situation, such as divorce or untimely widowhood, which called for action. For all, the routines and tasks of everyday life were changing.

Internal Motives for Changing Directions in Midstream   One of the main motivating forces for change is forced relocation. If women make educational and occupational choices based on proximity as we saw in chapter 2, they also relinquish educational and occupational choices when they have to relocate in order to maintain the status quo in the marriage and family. In chapter 3 we saw that thirty-eight out of forty-five women relocated upon marrying, twenty-five to follow their husbands' jobs, nine to follow their husbands' educations and three to be with their husband's families.

Twenty-seven of the forty-five women interviewed moved more than once to follow their husbands' careers. Some moved as often as once every two years. One woman felt that "moving was her whole life." Moving, or being ready to pull up stakes on short notice constituted a crisis situation.

The women felt that their plans had been short-circuited. They could not follow a stepwise path to any kind of career for themselves even though 31 percent of the women had initially desired this at some point in marriage. These women were particularly frustrated. It was not a matter of wanting their husbands to accompany them as they followed the labor market to other cities. It was only that they could not seem to stay in one place long enough to accomplish anything, yet they saw their husbands achieving success in their careers. For many, watching their husbands succeed led them to feel that, although they had begun the marriage on a relatively equal basis with regard to education and occupation, their husbands had excelled in their professions while the women had merely helped them to succeed. This often triggered resentment and their own desire to reengage.

> I always knew wherever we were was temporary so my only salvation was when we stayed in one place for two and a half years. I was determined to finish school. It was very important to me not to have to start all over again . . . If I hadn't been pregnant at the time and hadn't had my daughter . . . and had gone to the university straight away, I could have finished. I never had time to finish. My husband's career always came first. He followed the straight route with his education which went well. He did it step by step. It was just perfect. He did it all the right way, he's highly qualified. There was no compromising. I made all the compromises all through our married life.

Some were devastated by unwanted moves. During early marriage moving and pregnancy often went hand in hand. Having babies seemed to fill lonely gaps.

After the childbearing years, moves meant Newcomers Clubs, PTA, and social interaction with husbands' friends. For most women the loneliness of the moves was a recurrent nightmare and making friends was difficult. Each woman developed her own methods for adjusting to new communities.

> I moved to California. In the beginning the changes were brought about by the differences in life style as compared to Minnesota and being separated from the rest of my family and friends. The first step was becoming friends with a neighbor, actually with several neighbors, but very close to one of them. The second, I would say, was going to PTA meetings and meeting parents of the children's classmates and the third was social interchange with my husband's friends through his job.

Another woman relates her methods of adjustment:

> After the first move to our first house, I would seek out some type of organization – Newcomers, Junior Women's Club – something of this nature where I would meet other women that were having the same kind of circumstances that I was, just another adult to

talk to. I've always been involved with some sort of volunteering in any city we've lived in and then, as the children got into school, there would be PTA and other school-related activities which I would become involved in in each community. And with each move you have to go through the process of getting doctors and dentists and those exciting things too.

Women usually grew weary of being "camp followers" after a number of moves. This was particularly true as children began to enter their teenage years. In the beginning it seemed clear, however, that moving meant moving up for husbands, and wives benefited through added income.

The first move was very significant for me. Our son was one year old. My husband had just graduated from medical school and he was doing his internship so it was a very significant time professionally for me because I was a camp follower. It was very significant for me because it was the first time I had been away from my family, my parents, so that very intense relationship was subverted by my moving across the country, so essentially it was the first time I was on my own.

It was only when wives began to pursue external goals that they became angered by the moves. Some were mildly distressed and disappointed. Others saw the moves as their husband's methods of sabotaging their goals. Ambivalence was the dominant attitude.

I knew whatever furthered his career furthered my way of living and furthered me to do more and as I said he was always supportive for me to do it . . . I handled the money and it left him free to pursue his career.

Did you enjoy the moves?

I looked forward to all of them perhaps with the exception of this last one and that was because I was so close to completing my degree and looking forward to some sort of a life of my own in an area where I had become really a part of the community. I was on the school board and had an identity there which sort of vanished.

The case of the vanishing identity cropped up again and again. The women grew frustrated at "being somebody's wife and somebody's mother" and sought personal goals. They wanted to "put a name on" what they did, a label which was not solely a title in relation to other people.

With each move, their husbands achieved more and more. With each move, the women started again, constantly replenishing their supply of friends, constantly introducing themselves to new neighbors, constantly trying to find a doctor who had time to take care of one more family. In short, moves were good for husbands and bad for wives.

The second major factor which influenced women's motivation to make a transition was the Shrinking Circle. Children had taken up a good deal of time throughout the Expanding Circle Stage, the Peak Stage and the Full House Plateau and as they began to leave the nest, the women experienced role loss. They sought meaning to fill the voids left in the children's wake. If they were not yet directly involved in the Shrinking Circle Stage, they began to anticipate the trouble it would bring. Thinking about this period and possible alternatives usually began as early as when the last child was born.

The similarity between moving or anticipating a move and the Shrinking Circle or anticipating the Shrinking Circle is remarkable. In either case, women's identity undergoes a dramatic change which causes them to reevaluate and reorganize their priorities. Often, this implies allocating a different valuation to various roles played or tasks undertaken.

Reassigning value to tasks and routines is a symptom of the transition period. It is a manifestation of the Identity/Integrity Crisis. Reassessing worth can be conceptualized as "rewriting" one's personal history or "remapping." For example, these women often altered their perceptions of housework as they began their transition:

> I spent at least sixty hours a week on housework [before returning to college]. But then, you know, when you've got all day to do something, it takes you longer too because you're not pressured into a schedule. You don't have to be anywhere at any certain time and I think I was overcleaning a lot of times because I thought this is what I was supposed to be doing. So, I'd be doing things that maybe didn't have to be done.

She was not alone in her reevaluation of housework:

> See, what's funny about it is . . . that housework expands to fill the time available. Oh, it fits my category so perfectly to say this

because I wasn't getting that much done, but, yet, I spent a hell
of a lot of time either doing it or worrying about the fact that
I wasn't doing it. I would have trouble estimating how much
time I was actually working on housework before coming back
to school . . . probably fifty hours a week . . . I certainly like the
way I'm living now a lot better.

External Motives for Transition   Women's desires to fulfill themselves
outside of marriage are not the only sources of motivation to assume
new roles in adult life. Divorce or widowhood often leaves women
financially unstable.

For these women, financial stability implies finding work which they
can undertake for extended periods of time and which will supply a
living wage for themselves and their children. As we shall observe in
chapter 6, divorce or widowhood usually cuts the total annual family
income in half.

The motive becomes a matter of economics. Money is the driving force.
Necessity outweighs the internal drive to achieve.

In sum, we have discovered two primary sources of motivation for
entering into a transition period in adult life for these reengaging women.
The first was a search for continuous meaningful activity which would
replace lost roles or provide greater depth to the existing roles in women's
lives. The second was financial. Due to unforeseen rearrangement of the
familial structure, the women found themselves in the position of needing
money in order to insure a standard of living within which they could
be comfortable. For some women, the need for meaning and the need
for money were indivisible. Making money, in and of itself, provided meaning for some women. They viewed money as power. Access to their own
money gave them control over their own futures in a familial situation
which they perceived as unstable or inequitable. It gave them stock in
the future.

Looking Ahead

What are your plans for the future?

I've given that a good deal of thought. I feel like I want to work
part-time because I feel it is of utmost importance that someone's
home when the children get home from school. I just feel that that
is really mandatory because our world today is very . . . There's

too many things out there that kids can turn to if they don't have someone at home to turn to and I want to be the one that's close to my children . . . So part-time work is my goal for the time. When my children completely leave, I think I would like to work full time. When the last one is gone, and she's gone to school or to work or to get married or whatever, I would like to work full-time but up until then I would like to go to school. I know basically where my interests are but I would like to apply that to a job, a job that would fit into those interests.

Another said:

I'm going to have trouble answering that question because my husband and I feel that we're in a transition period. We're reevaluating our standards and our ideas and our goals. It changes from day to day at this point. I know this transition period will settle down into something.

Plans for the future may unfold over a period of years. An immediate change does not usually occur as a result of one particular experience. For most of the women in our sample, the Identity/Integrity Crisis was the result of entering into or anticipating the Shrinking Circle Stage. It was the result of wanting "something more" for themselves as their children needed them less and less often.

The most typical response to questions concerning the future was one describing a gradual transition from motherhood to career or "meaningful" job:

I would like to work two or three half days a week if I could find a job where I could go in when my kids go to school and work for four or five hours a couple of times a week so I'm only gone during their school hours. I would like that because I really enjoy being home when the kids get home from school.

Was there a specific point when you started thinking about this job seriously?

I never thought about it as a possible reality until after my last baby was born. I had thought about going back to school and doing something that year or during the time I was pregnant but I don't think it became specific until after the baby was born.

School became a step on that pathway. It provided the springboard for goal clarification. The women could focus on the future more clearly when they felt that they were already on their way to meeting their goals.

The Push to Career   Seventy-five percent of the women interviewed were motivated to pursue a career. Seventy-eight percent were motivated to complete a college degree. The period of transition was characterized by a high degree of future orientation which represents a dramatic shift in attitude as compared to the present-oriented attitudes of the early marital years.

Nineteen women sought a career as a way of obtaining their own independence, as a way of finding out what their career potential might be and working toward it. They wanted satisfaction in the sense of "meaning" and they wanted "freedom" to contribute to their families financially and to develop their own contacts with the "outside world" apart from husbands and children.

> I knew that I needed something . . . What I had done was I had checked out what I saw as the options for me according to the pattern my mother had laid out. "This is what a grown-up woman does." Well, I had done all that and I still wasn't satisfied and so it was sort of vague. I didn't know exactly what I wanted but I knew I wanted something more than that and that feeling just kept getting stronger and stronger . . . I wanted something serious in my life too.

Another woman explains her transition to a career orientation this way:

> I was feeling a great deal of frustration because I knew that I could do so many other things besides scrub the kitchen floor and fix another meal . . . I did not ever have a clear picture of myself doing something . . . I had this anger and this frustration and sense of powerlessness because I couldn't really pinpoint anything out there that I wanted to do.

The sense of frustration many of these women felt often resulted from a feeling of powerlessness in the world external to their families. Some women felt trapped by their lack of power to move outside of their home environment. There were frequent reports of "cabin fever" and conceptualizations of the home as prison. This lack of control became a catalyst for women's desire to have a career:

> I started thinking about a career when I was in New York and couldn't go anywhere after I had my first baby. I got cabin fever and started thinking about it. What am I going to do? Well, I knew I should be prepared to do something in case I *had* to work and I *knew* I didn't want to work at something I didn't like so I really started trying to discover what I would like if I had to work or wanted to work.

Some women recognized their career needs as a question of power, but they were careful about their language, careful about the wording of their responses:

> I seriously thought about going back into a career when my youngest child was seven or eight years old. It was a restlessness with . . . Well, as I think the counselor at the Women's Center voiced it, she said, you've always been so busy, so busy that I couldn't settle to a day of seeing people off to school and hours free, you know, I needed to be continually busy. The amount of canning I needed to do was cutting down and I was no longer sewing very much. The girls had taken over all their own. I sewed very little for the last because he preferred knit shirts to smooth ones and I just wanted to be busy and to feel needed. Maybe, to a certain extent, it was a feeling of importance or of power. Power is a touchy word to use because I don't mean it in the autocratic sense. And then, to some extent, a feeling of I'm going to need to contribute if we're going to have more than a bare minimum retirement, if we're going to be able to do things rather than just be at the poverty level.

Others were more direct in their desires:

> I love making money, just the challenge of making it. I love to make things succeed. I will feel that I have arrived when I can have a business that makes money . . . I love that power. It's validation and it's power.

"Independence," "power," "personal satisfaction," "stimulation" and "validation" were the reasons most often given for seeking a job or career. A few people wanted to pursue careers so they could be a "good role model" for their children. The remainder wanted to fill up time or were looking for a preventative financial measure in case of widowhood or divorce.

When the reentry women summarized their main reasons for returning
to school, the reasons they gave were most often identical to those they
provided as the rationale for their pending entry into the labor market.
They usually provided concise lists of reasons of which the following
were typical:

1. to leave the boring humdrum civilian life to get into academia
2. self-improvement
3. to make a living
4. to accumulate knowledge, expertise and be effective

1. to get the right job
2. to make money
3. love school
4. self-betterment
5. intellectual stimulation

1. to separate from family
2. to learn about self
3. to pursue a career

1. to develop and mature
2. self-nurturance

1. to do something important
2. serious purpose, meaning
3. to contribute to society

1. to escape isolation, make friends
2. mental stimulation
3. emotional satisfaction
4. to become more wise and cultured

Three-fourths of the women interviewed considered themselves to be
on a career track. They sought meaning, fulfillment and methods of
securing their futures financially.

The Mid-life Drive for Money and Meaning   The net effect of this mid-
life drive for money and meaning was a kind of cognitive dissonance which
was manifested in a reevaluation of the wife/mother role complex. The
structure of everyday routines began to undergo change as the women
sought control over their own futures. They had seen their husbands
progressing in their careers in a step by step fashion and they perceived
themselves to be continually starting over in a haphazard way. The numerous moves and focus on children had elicited an other-orientation on
the part of the women but they grew weary of always "being the one to

adjust." Flexibility became a dirty word as ambivalence grew and the women began to demand "something for themselves." In general, this "demand" began as a "vague feeling" and escalated into a "need." Concern about the future and planning long-term goals was the result of the transition period. Reengagement at schools which would allow these women a better foothold in the job market was the logical outcome. Yet, even in reengaging, identity problems are perpetuated. The very terminology utilized by programs drawing women into schools implies that they have been disengaged from a culturally potent role. Ironically, women are told that they have been disengaged during the long stretch of time when they have been nurturing their children. This is the time when women are most involved in fulfilling their duties as wives and mothers. They have dutifully carried out the mandate for wife- and motherhood, work which seems to hold little value in the eyes of employers and teachers. It seems to be further cause for reevaluation: Women see their mothering duties as temporally limited and they bide their time until the point when they feel they can terminate portions of the motherhood role with a clear conscience.

Reengaging as a Case of Biographical Rupture If to disengage is to become detached from social contacts and responsibilities, then to reengage is to become actively involved in contacts and responsibilities again. This implies that engagement has occurred previously, followed by a period of disengagement, followed by reengagement. It appears that this engagement-disengagement-reengagement process corresponds with specific stages in women's adult life cycle. Prior to marriage the women interviewed were somewhat inner-oriented, that is, pursuing personal goals. However, as it became more important to them to find a mate and to build a family, they became increasingly oriented toward satisfying others' needs. As they became wives and entered the Expanding Circle Stage, this other orientation became legitmated and institutionalized.

"Vanishing Identities," caused by relocating numerous times and the restructuring of the family system caused by the Shrinking Circle, divorce or widowhood cause women to redefine appropriate occupations as major life projects. What does this mean for women who were socialized to believe that marriage and motherhood would be the primary tasks of adult life?

Initially, let us look at the meaning of maintaining a particular reality. Reality is internalized through the processes of primary and secondary socialization. During primary socialization, before entering school, the individual internalizes what is perceived as the inevitable, abstracting from the roles and attitudes of concrete significant others. For women, primary socialization has meant learning the traditional roles of motherhood.

In secondary socialization, school women have been tracked into general areas or women's fields and girls emerge from high school with less ambition to succeed in the paid work world than their male counterparts.

The drive to marry and the motherhood mandate are upheld by women through subjective reflection and social objectification. Usually, until women enter into the Peak Stage, the symbolic universe of family remains meaningful and the reality is self-maintaining. This reality is maintained through carrying out the routine tasks of everyday life. These routines are the essence of institutionalization. Thus the reality of motherhood is institutionalized as the woman enters into the Expanding Circle Stage and that reality becomes self-maintaining. It is reaffirmed in her interactions with others. It follows that, as long as the individual remains within this plausible structure, she feels any doubts of this reality are unfounded (Cf. Berger and Luckmann, 1966).

Problems with reality maintenance may arise, as we have seen, from two main sources. One is internal. Women seek an added dimension of meaning to their lives. The other problem is external. Women are forced to alter their perceptions of what they felt would be their major adult roles by divorce, widowhood or financial instability. Often it is a combination of internal and external variables which cause women to begin to redefine or to remap. Reengaging women, as a group, experience problems in evaluating the consistency of what is expected of them from the outside. They also reevaluate what they want for themselves as a reflection of what they perceive coming from the outside.

In 1965, Hans Toch pointed out that individuals can live with inconsistencies as long as the inconsistencies do not come into direct contact with each other. Beliefs are safe as long as they are not put to the test. For example, an adult may be most secure against change if he or she has been socialized with consistent beliefs and if those beliefs are representative of situations or experiences that he or she will be most likely to encounter.

In contemporary America, the belief in the sanctity of the marriage and motherhood roles has come into direct conflict with the reality of financial and emotional needs for women. The divorce rate is rising and the economic situation is tightening. It is no longer plausible for most women to consider the pursuit of wifehood and motherhood as the exclusive reality. This calls for a reorientation.

Switching worlds or switching realities requires resocialization. The new plausibility structure is mediated by significant others, the news media and so on. Thus, women's subjective reality is transformed and this whole sequence of transformation is legitimated as women take part in reengagement programs. Peter Berger and Thomas Luckmann (1966) have called this process "biographical rupture."

Biographical rupture involves straightening out a discrepancy between what one is socialized to believe and the actual situations that arise. For women, this biographical rupture has involved inconsistencies between discrepant worlds—that of home and family and that of career.

The reality base for resocialization, particularly with regard to reengagement is the present environment. Options which present themselves in close geographical proximity can become the basis for reevaluation or reorganization of one's life or one's priorities. For example, in the present sample, 69 percent (n=31) of the women chose the school at which they reentered on the basis of present location. Only 4 percent (n=2) chose the institution on the basis of its academic merit. The schools were, in most cases, convenient options for women in the midst of a transition to consider.

The Reengaging Woman as Horatia Alger   We have been looking at a crisis situation in women's lives wherein reentry women have undergone a transformation from day-by-day contingency-oriented individuals to future-oriented career seekers. Though it should be noted that the women are energized and excited about their reengagement, it would also be misleading to stop the discussion here.

All of these women were headed toward a career. A large majority of them were interested in going into the social sciences, particularly in the areas of psychology and sociology, areas in which they felt that their age and life experience might be an advantage in "helping people." Twelve women were interested in the humanities, in which they hoped to carve out independent careers. Only six people mentioned any form of business.

It is interesting that none of the women mentioned careers in science or engineering, areas of technological development or the professions. They have instead chosen fields which are most consistent with the "nurturant" or "expressive" female role. These "helping" fields are relatively easy to move in and out of as family responsibilities demand.

Perhaps this is yet another extension of the contingency orientation. It seems to be at least partially due to the Horatia Alger Syndrome, which was introduced in chapter 2. Laurie Davidson Cummings (1977) found that college women perceived the pursuit of success to be based on the idea of merit and luck: struggling upward with a benevolent sponsor. Women see an unproblematic future as long as they can find a supportive husband. Reentry women seem to fall into this syndrome as well in that they feel that they can "struggle" upwards, but not too far, if they choose a field in which their age and circumstances will not have a direct bearing.

The Temporality Hypothesis   It seems in order to introduce yet another component of the contingency orientation in wives and mothers. Re-engaging women seem to base their career decisions on stages in their lives which relate to their roles in childcare. Thus, the idea of the temporality of their plans becomes exceedingly important in studying their achievement. This factor of timing will be called the Temporality Hypothesis.

Not only do we need to take into account women's marriage and fertility plans and early marital fertility behavior when we are studying the status attainment process, as hypothesized by William Falk and Arthur Cosby (1975), but we must also take into account women's mid-life participation in the educational and occupational arenas.

This variable should be considered when examining the status attainment process for women. We need to assess the temporal nature of women's plans and the extent to which orientations toward goals depend on the changing stages of their families and on changes in familial structure.

In the next chapter, we will see that women's families remain quite significant as reactionary entities when women begin to change the rules of the game in the transition period.

6
Setbacks

Even when college women are career salient, they still expect to marry, bear children and provide emotional and perhaps financial support for a husband struggling upward in a job or career. College women today generally perceive career as a job not superceding family duties in importance, thus it becomes part of a total life style which women expect to enter.

There is much evidence which points to the conclusion that career-oriented college women are not fundamentally different in their outlook from college women who are not gearing up for a career. For both groups, the perceived adult role complex still involves marriage and family.

We have explored, to some extent, the meaning of marriage in women's lives. Marriage provides an identity and a role complex which are congruent with the stereotype of the wife "as supporter, comforter, backstage manager, home maintainer, and main rearer of children" (Cf. Papanek, 1973). Women have traditionally expected, upon marriage, to enter into a two-person career which establishes a particular status quo in the family system. Interrupting the normal functioning of this

93

equilibrium by making a move which alters the expected relationships within the family can cause discomfort and can sometimes be devastating to family members. This chapter examines reactions in women's immediate environments as they strive to integrate new roles. We begin by exploring what is initially expected upon entering marriage.

The Two-Person Career

Hanna Papanek (1973) defines what she calls the "two-person single career." It involves a particular combination of roles which ensue as a result of formal and informal institutional demands which are placed on both members of a married couple by the agency for which the husband is employed. This is a prevalent pattern in the American middle class.

In a situation in which the nature of access to education is becoming more equitable, the two-person career often presents a dilemma for wives. Women are becoming more educated, yet the demands of their husbands' jobs often require that they participate on a secondary level, for example, by entertaining the husband's colleagues, or more subtly, by maintaining the home environment so that the husband can be maximally productive.

The two-person career involves a three way relationship between husband, wife and employer. As Papanek points out, these relationships, where the wife is involved, are not by specific choice of the employer or of the wife, but rather they come about as a result of the wife's sexual, economic and emotional bonds with her husband.

Because the demands of this three way interaction are generally very involved, wives may often feel a certain reluctance toward developing careers at a level for which their education has prepared them (Cf. Papanek, 1973). Further, they may be reluctant to attain the education for which they have the potential in the first place. Very career-oriented women who find themselves in the traditional two-person career pattern may establish jobs or careers for themselves which in some manner are able to incorporate the demands of the husband's job, for example, through part-time work or working with their husband. In this way, the dilemma is partially resolved.

The majority of women, however, do not attempt to resolve the dilemma or perhaps do not perceive it as a dilemma. Helena Lopata discovered that the most highly educated women were most likely to be interested in their husbands' jobs and the problems and social relationships involved therein (Cf. Papanek, 1973).

As a result of these patterns which women have expected as a component of adult life, women have traditionally sought men whom they felt would be good providers. We have seen that women tend to "marry-up" with regard to education and that this pattern may have become increasingly predominant throughout this century. Marriage becomes a path to social mobility for women. This is true educationally and occupationally.

Further, the educational and occupational attrition rates for women have been shown to be related to family commitments. Whether or not a woman enters school or the job market also appears to be related to family commitments. For example, Saul Feldman (1973) found that the husbands of graduate students are likely to have a graduate education themselves. He attributes this to the fact that, since it has been deemed unacceptable in our society for women to dominate their husbands in any way, women are not free to pursue advanced degrees if their husbands have not done so as well. He found that these differences with regard to education in married pairs hold true regardless of age. It is just as true for younger women as for women over forty.

When women do enter graduate school, they are much more likely than men to give "intellectual stimulation" as the reason. Men tend to state that they are in graduate school for economic reasons (Cf. Feldman, 1973).

When all of these points are taken together, the expectations for division of labor in the marital relationship become clear. Husband equals breadwinner and wife equals supportive personality and mother to the children. Obviously, this is an oversimplification in light of individual differences but, by and large, this basic pattern holds in the American middle class. When wives who have performed the role of emotional support in the family system begin to ask for this themselves, problems arise. Alterations in the roles wives perform or in the way they perform specific roles call for alteration in the roles of other family members. This is also the case for women who are single heads of households. A change-oriented action elicits a reaction from others who are affected by that change.

When women are caught in the throes of change in their own lives and in the lives of their families, they are heavily influenced by the network surrounding them and the responses they encounter in their environment.

The Effects of Change on Pair Satisfaction

A medical doctor, Hugh Drummond (1979) states that women who have never married experience more satisfaction than married women. He notes that married women have higher rates of mental and physical illness and shorter life spans than single women. Married men, on the other hand, live longer and experience fewer illnesses than single men. The result, he adds, is that "marriage seems to be good for men and bad for women." And with a touch of humor, he says, "The obvious public health conclusion from this is that men should marry other men and leave women alone."

Nonetheless, we all acknowledge that the institution of marriage will persist even though it may be undergoing some subtle changes. The dual career family is becoming more prevalent in our society and this form of family life apparently puts pressure on husbands of working women. Though studies have found that working wives experience more satisfaction with their roles, the husbands of these working wives have more trouble relating to them (Cf. Burke and Weir, 1976). Husbands experience increased worry over housing and money problems when their wives work. They are more likely to feel "in a rut" and they have difficulties in communicating with and showing affection for their wives. They experience less happiness with marriage than husbands of housewives, in addition to poorer mental and physical health. They are more likely to describe themselves as worriers and their spirits as low (Cf. Burke and Weir, 1976). Ronald Burke and Tamara Weir (1976) have provided several explanations for these husbands' attitudes.

Initially, they claim, when a wife works outside the home the husband loses part of his support system in that the time a wife can give to his emotional, social and physical needs is altered. When the wife tries to integrate her work and home responsibilities, the husband loses the satisfaction and comfort he has come to expect "when the wife functions as a kind of servant." The husband may be undertaking more of what he once considered to be woman's work in the home in addition to the tasks which were traditionally his in the household. Further he is "put in the position of playing a supportive role to his wife's ambitions and personal goals."

> His central position in the family is eroded, and with it his former dominance and power . . . The picture that emerges is one of the husband experiencing a reduction in important services, an increase in his burden of responsibilities and a loss of his special status in the family . . . the husband may have to deal with a diminished sense of self-worth in his dual-role relations with the family, whereas, the wife's sense of self-worth is likely to be enhanced (Burke and Weir, 1976).

The dual career family seems to imply contradictions of status for husbands and wives. Advocates of the dual career family model have recognized the barriers the family creates for women's personal achievement but they have tended to underestimate or ignore the supportive role of the family in the personal achievement of men (Cf. Hunt and Hunt, 1977). If women are to succeed at careers, perhaps they need the same elements of support. Dual career families suffer strains in that there is no supportive partner to provide socioemotional backing and there are problems as well with childcare and domestic work overload. In outlining stresses of dual career families, Janet Hunt and Larry Hunt (1977) mention the following:

1. Demands on the couple's time and the absence of a traditional wife to perform socioemotional functions create increased tension.
2. Strain in the family results from changing values, particularly concerning conflicting cultural ethics of work and duty, on the one hand, and fun and personal freedom on the other.
3. Careerism for wives does not offer women the life style men have enjoyed because they cannot fully delegate their family responsibilities which may result in role conflict.
4. Parenting becomes less attractive as an option which makes the motherhood role seem increasingly obsolete as defined in homebound terms.

Most studies concur that the attitude of husbands and "society in general" is negative with regard to women's working. Candida Peterson and James Peterson (1975) suggest that, furthermore, "the attitude against the wife's greater relative earnings is not as pervasive as the attitude against paternal child care."

Not only do women face obstacles in society, they face them in their own families. This seems to be particularly the case for reentry women. Why?

Angelica Brennan (1979) and Lita Linzer Schwartz (1977) both document marital tension created by wives' entering college. Brennan found that significant numbers of reengaging women experienced increased tension with husbands since reentry, anxiety over their husbands' wanting to change jobs or lifestyles, concern over changes in their marital sex life and many women felt that their husbands were critical of their return to school. All of these factors were less critical for community college students than for returning graduate students.

Lita Schwartz (1977) quotes Matina Horner as remarking:

> No one ever seriously objects to a woman's education or intellectual development, provided its objective is to make her a more entertaining companion and a more enlightened, and thus better, wife and mother. Only when her objective is an independent personal career does a problem arise.

She asks why this is true. What home variables might account for the problem?

> If she [the wife] achieves success, whether academic, financial, or in professional recognition, does this pose a threat to her husband's ego? If her star is rising while his hangs by a thread, is at a plateau, or is falling, does he resent the situation? Does he perceive her activity as competition with him? Can he rejoice with her when she attains a goal?

The bottom line of all these investigations and commentaries is that when women pursue goals external to their roles as wives and mothers, husbands grow resentful. Though women may be accruing more satisfaction with life in general, husbands are becoming angry.

Husbands' Attitudes Toward Change   Out of the twenty-seven married women in the present sample, eighteen say that their husbands resent their participation in the academic environment. Twelve of these women claim that their student role is the source of much argument in their marriages. Only nine women felt that their husbands were supportive of their involvements outside of the home.

Their husbands had always expected them to keep the house clean and to have dinner on the table when they returned home from work. Over half of these women still had children living at home and it was not an easy task to work school into an already busy schedule, particularly when husbands were demanding.

How did they do it? Some women stated that they felt they may have been "overcleaning" in the past and that after they entered school they did not aspire to such a high degree of spotlessness.

Most of them, however, tried to live with a greater quantity of criticism coming from their husbands. The criticism was triggered by the women's falling down in what their husbands felt to be their primary role in the marriage. They were not performing up to par. Their husbands resented it when they spent less time on housework and less time in the house.

Most husbands did not buy the "overcleaning" explanation. Some of them expressed their feelings by "writing messages in the dust." Other husbands were more vocal about their contentions. Many women spoke similarly to this woman:

> He [my husband] makes snide little comments . . . why I'm not home when I'm supposed to be home and the dinners that are put on the table are "absolutely rancid," the house isn't picked up the way it's supposed to be and the washing isn't done exactly the day he thinks he needs something that he wants done. He feels like he's very abused . . . He's very threatened.

Another woman offers:

> School is always a source of argument. School is a threat. It's very damaging to his ego if I ever find out anything whereby he's made a mistake, you know, financially, or things that would delve into work. As long as I learn things that have nothing to do with how he might run his business or any other phase — I think what he would have liked would have been a lack of knowledge and a steady paycheck from me.

The two-thirds of the married women who have resentful husbands seem to feel that their husbands will not resent them if they do not deviate from their prescribed roles as housewives and mothers. When they deviate from this track, the husband's own sense of identity and security is threatened. "My husband has been disinterested [in my school work]. I think he doesn't want to know about my school because it's threatening." Why is he threatened?

> Why is he threatened? I think because he feels that I might find something better by going to school than being at home. He also thinks I'm going to run away with somebody else. He thinks there's men over there that I would have to talk to. He's really insecure about it.

Husbands "seem bitter." They "can't see the point" of their wives going to school. They feel their wives are "wasting their time." They do not want their wives encroaching on what they feel is their domain: breadwinner and liaison with the outside world, knowledgeable about events which take place outside of the home. They do not like their wives' "attitudes." "He does not like my new 'liberated' attitude which I must admit I do to get a rise out of him and to expose him to what's going on in the world."

Husbands did not mind wives' outside involvement as long as it contributed to what they felt to be the familial goals, for example, if their wives were working while they were in school or if they were in a financial bind. The following comment was very typical:

> I started to think about pursuing a career in the last year and a half. I had thought that if I went back to work – I didn't think it was really much of a possibility because my husband is adamantly against it. As long as I was bringing in the income while he went to school it was okay.

Husbands' attitudes were more blatantly negative when they were directly faced with the absence of their wives at a time when they felt that they should be in the house. For most, night classes and weekend studying presented intense problems. If there seemed to be outward support and undercurrents of discontent on the part of the husbands, these were times when the discontent became manifest.

> He was deeply, deeply jealous, sick. I mean it was sick jealousy in the beginning and that has now changed. Basically he thinks my going back to school is terrific. Every now and then he gets scared. He used to have the classic problem that if he let go of me I might fly away . . . From time to time he has a real fear of what this might mean to him, what it might mean to our relationship and to him. The thing that really bothers him is that I have two night classes but that's it. He will be displeased about the inconvenience but I would be doing him a disservice if I paid attention to this.

Stresses grow when husbands' time with wives is interfered with.

> There's nothing like a stress time at school, finals . . . As a prime example, the day that he chose to announce that he thought it was never going to work and that we should separate, I was studying for finals. It's like the kids always get sick or your husband decides to be helpless and dependent and need you for everything he does that week. So it seems logical that our problems probably have something to do with school because I had been very available before that and then suddenly it's like "Don't bother me now, kid. I'm in the middle of studying for this exam!"

Husbands often felt that their leisure time with their wives was being infringed upon. David Jorgenson (1977) found that wife/mother employment is, in fact, inversely related to husband-wife leisure time. For wife/mother students we have seen that husbands resent it when their wives are not home in the evenings or are studying on weekends.

In a study of life stress and marital conflict, Charles Frederickson (1977) found that the incidence of marital dysfunction is greatest when one or both of the partners in the marriage have undergone a major life event which calls for an adjustment on the part of husband and/or wife. Examples of major life events mentioned by Frederickson include "revision of personal habits (dress, manners, associations)," "outstanding personal achievement," "spouse beginning or ceasing work outside the home," "major change in social activities (clubs, movies, visiting)" and "beginning or ceasing formal schooling," all of which may apply to re-engaging women and their families.

Yet if women do not change their activities as they age, they are very likely to experience alienation in their marriage (Cf. Beyer and Whitehurst, 1976). Mary Alice Beyer and Robert N. Whitehurst (1976) found that women who have been married over fifteen years have more negative self concepts than younger married women. Further, this team discovered that over the life cycle men and women experience a reversal in positive and negative meanings associated with the marriage. Older men are more satisfied whereas their wives are less satisfied. They attribute this to the fact that events within and outside of the marriage are markedly different and have markedly different meanings for husbands than for wives and vice versa. Men seem to be more influenced by events before and after there are children while women are more influenced by the presence of children (Cf. Beyer and Whitehurst, 1976). Children may be seen as the major "crusade" (see chapter 4) and when they are gone, women need to replace the mothering activities with other kinds of activities or run the risk of experiencing a great deal of alienation as they age.

Husbands apparently do not see this as a problem. Perhaps marital communication reflects the macropolitics of sexism in our society. Larry Alsbrook (1976) asks:

> Could it be possible that the interpersonal dynamics of marital relationships have the class and caste characteristics of sexism in society at large? Would an analysis of communication patterns of conflicted marriages reveal a process of discrimination against the women?

After carrying out a three year study on this issue, he concludes in the affirmative.

At any rate, husbands want the status quo preserved and they have various ways of seeing that the marriage remains intact only under certain specified conditions. Through fluctuations in their physical and mental health, they manipulate their wives' behavior.

When wives gain control of their personal futures, husbands feel out of control of their own marital futures. If they "let them go, they might fly away."

> It's very difficult for my husband because he comes from a family that . . . His mother is extremely domineering and he hated it. It's very hard for him because he thinks any time a woman is assertive that's aggressive because that's what his mother was . . . When I went to school we started communicating for the first time in our married life. I started saying how I really felt . . . He still reluctantly would like to know in his mind that I'm securely fastened to that toilet seat but he's not going to jeopardize our marriage by saying that's the way it has to be. He is coming around a little bit.

And many women do find their marriages in jeopardy. Several of the women who were divorced mentioned off the cuff that they felt their going back to school had something to do with it either on their part or on their husband's part. Either their worlds were expanding and their husbands were threatened by this or they were outgrowing their husbands as a result of their outside involvements. Sometimes their husband's resentment made them all the more determined to obtain a degree. One divorced woman said:

> He literally smothered me because everything was for him and he knew that if he said "I don't like the meetings you're going to, I don't like your student involvement in such and such an organization" that I would sit back and say, "Well, my marriage and my family's more important" . . . immediately that I would get out of that organization, immediately stop. But those were threats he always held over my head and they always worked. Not anymore! I'm *definitely* going back to school and I'm *definitely* finishing.

Wives' Attitudes Toward Husbands   Only four women responded to their husbands' anger with resentment. Ten related to their husbands as they always had, but twelve women felt increasingly positive feelings toward their husbands. They felt more equal and more understanding of their husband's status and position in the world. They appreciated his knowledge more and felt more fulfilled in the relationship when they were involved in school. Most of the women who experienced more satisfaction with their husbands had something resembling the following to say:

> I look at my husband's profession now in a totally different way. I really can kind of appreciate what he's doing and also his knowledge and the way he can do things. I respect him a lot more.

And respect leads to equality.

> My husband would put me down a lot. He'd say "You're so lucky to have this nice big house and you don't have to work." And I would always say to myself, "Yeah, he's right, I don't have to work." He said, "You don't have anything to complain about. You shouldn't complain because you've got it made" and I would think, "Yeah, he's right, we don't have any financial worries." What's wrong with me? My kids are healthy, we don't have any problems there. I was wondering why am I so depressed? That was how I was a year ago and now I have more opinions about things. I just feel that whenever he says something I have an answer to come back rather than to agree with him, just putting myself down more. I feel like there's some conversation going on from my end now, more equal intellectually.

Most of these women felt that their relationships with their husbands had much more potential to be strong and secure. As they became more satisfied with themselves and their abilities, they became more satisfied and interested in their marriages. Many of them, for the first time, saw their husbands in a "new light." The relationship had taken on more depth, more meaning. They felt "freer in the relationship" and had a "positive new image" of their husbands. They were finding ways to "be more creative and communicative" in the marriage and they were more aware of the type of pressure their husbands were under.

On the other hand, they felt more equal and were "willing to stand up against" their husbands in a way that they would not have done before they entered school. They were more aware of discrimination against women in society at large and more aware of their rights in society and, particularly, in marriage.

Essentially, as the level of satisfaction women feel with their marriage increases as they pursue external goals, the level of satisfaction experienced by their husbands decreases.

Children and Change

We have seen that these women's primary involvement during adult life was with children. Because of the intensity of the relationship between mother and child, the attitudes and opinions of the children of these women had an effect on the choices they made with regard to activities outside of the family locus.

Children's Reactions to Mother as Student   Lita Schwartz (1977) comments that mothers who become students must be prepared for various reactions from their offspring. She asks:

> Can they accept her in multiple roles? Are they resentful of the external demands on their mother's time and attention? Are they proud or overwhelmed by her achievements? What effect do her achievements have on their school or work efforts?

By way of answering her own questions, Schwartz notes that women must plan extensively in order to have time and energy for family pursuits while going to school so that children do not become resentful and lose respect for their mothers.

Additionally, Angelica Brennan (1979) finds that women attending community college experience much worry over their children and increased tension with them. Women graduate students also experience this tension but to a lesser extent.

For our sample, the reactions of children to the changing roles of their mothers varied. Of the thirty-six women who had children living at home, twelve mothers thought that their children were supportive of their endeavors outside of the home. They were "proud" of their mothers' accomplishments, they saw them as "good role model(s)," they were "excited" about their mothers' interests, and they had "more in common" with their mothers with regard to school work. Many of the children enjoyed their new independence and were happy about the fact that their mothers were no longer "hovering" over them.

Some women felt that their children were indifferent to their activities and one woman expressed disappointment over this fact because she had "hoped they would be proud of her."

A few women said that their children's moods changed. On some occasions they expressed delight in their mothers' activities away from home and on other occasions, they resented "the times when mother was not there."

Eight women sensed distress signals coming from their children. They felt that their children were resentful. They wanted "to do fun things" with their mothers. They did not want them away from home at night. They did not want them studying on the weekends and they wanted a companion for watching television. For these resentful children, time was most often the issue. They wanted their mothers to spend more time with them and they felt that spending time with them was her job. Most of them were not comfortable with their mothers in "multiple roles." "I think they feel that I do a lot . . . I think that they only think in terms of time. How much time can I spend with them?" Another woman remarked:

> They aren't supportive. I'm busy and I'm doing homework and I don't have a lot of time. But it will be okay again once I'm out of school. You know they're self-centered like most kids.

Women tended to stress the temporariness of their outside involvements to their children. They told their children that there would be more time in the summer, during vacations or as soon as they graduated.

> They don't like my being busy all the time. They tell me that I'm always busy and we don't have time to do the fun things that we used to and I tell them it's temporary, that it won't always be like this, but I need their help.

Yet because eleven of these women with children at home were divorced and found themselves in the situation of having to go to work, there was no choice. Only three divorced women felt that their children were supportive of their student activities. Twice this number felt that their children were resentful but some of these children, though angry, did understand the importance of what their mothers were doing. In other words, they tolerated their mother's behavior even though they would have preferred to have her at home.

Mothers' Attitudes Toward Children   If a changing familial situation elicited a reaction from children, likewise did it inspire mothers' new attitudes toward children.

Only thirteen women felt that their attitudes toward their children had not changed as a result of their involvements. The remaining thirty-one mothers expressed a positive change in their attitudes. Eleven women were more understanding and patient. They felt that this was because they had other things to think about and thus were not entirely consumed with their children's behavior. In addition, they felt that they understood the problems their children were having at school to a much greater extent. They were more empathetic.

> I'm more understanding about my children. Well, instead of being right on their case when something doesn't go right and when they forget their books at school and they come running back . . . Since I've been coming to school, I've forgotten my books. Sometimes it's just hard to remember. You forget that when you're in school, you have forty-four little tiny details to remember all the time. I think I'm more tolerant of things they do that are wrong and I try to be a little less judgmental and critical. It's easy when you're home watching all these things go on all the time and just sit there and be judge of it all. I think when you're out there too and experiencing some of this, then, you know how it is and you don't jump down their neck every time something doesn't go quite right.

Another woman offered this:

> I'm much more understanding of what my children are going through because I'm going through something out of the house. There were times before that I would get angry and think, Well everybody else gets to leave and everybody else gets to do something and everybody else has their own life and I'm left to have all the dishes done, to work, and everybody else just gets to come back and enjoy it. I don't feel that way anymore. I really feel that each one of us has our own thing.

In general, the mothers felt more equal to their children and felt a much greater depth of respect for them. This was particularly true for those women with grown children who quipped, tongue in cheek, that their children "weren't as smart as they thought."

The women with young children found themselves enjoying their children's company more, as did those with older children. There was more to talk about, more focus on the world outside of the family. Many women expressed that they had found a new "delight" in their relationship with their children. They "treasured" their children more. One woman felt that going to school was like "being turned loose in a circus" and she could offer everything she had seen to her children. She had become more of a teacher to them. Others felt this way as well and they often saw themselves as positive role models for their children.

I didn't want my children to consider my going back to school as just another thing that I was involved with. I wanted them to be aware of what I was doing and why I was doing it, what it meant to their father and their mother. I wanted my daughter to be very clear in what was going on and I wanted my son to be very aware of what was going on from a feminist standpoint . . . It's neat for my son to see me going through some of the things that he is going through scholastically and to talk about those things, what works for me, what doesn't work for me, handy hints for studying, those kind of things.

Her son began to take his school work more seriously and he became more and more supportive of his mother's involvements. He began to understand, as did other children, that mothers have potential for outside involvements just as he himself did.

Whether the children of these women experienced positive or negative feelings about their mothers going to college, the mothers overwhelmingly experienced a positive change of attitude toward their children. Interactions with children became less a duty and more a chosen course of activity. The mothers began to seek their children as intellectual companions or as curious, intelligent and interested beings with whom they might share their "circus" of ideas.

Family Disruption and the High Cost of Leaving

In general, women enjoyed their families more upon becoming students. Outside involvements caused them to reevaluate their relationships with their families and to rediscover the positive aspects of belonging to a family unit. They rediscovered their husbands and remembered why they had chosen them as partners in marriage and their children became more of a delight. Nonetheless, as we have seen, husbands and children did not necessarily share the women's feelings about their new station in life. They were often resentful and, in a few cases, outside involvements on the part of wives was a major factor in bringing about a divorce.

When this woman enrolled in school she found her bags packed for her and stacked on the front porch:

My husband was opposed [to my going to school] and said, "You can get another job, but you can't go to college." And I said, "But the only kind of job I can get in this area is secretarial shit. I can be more than that. I can be so much more than I've been in this life here. And I need to do that, I need to find out what else I can be," and I went into this: "I've put sixteen years of my life into letting you explore your potential. You've become a pretty incredible man from when I knew you. You've done a lot."

Her husband's success triggered her desire to develop her talents, but it was to the detriment of her marriage. Her husband could not tolerate her in roles that were unfamiliar to him. He wanted the status quo preserved and this couple ended up divorced.

Many women mentioned that they were going to school at the risk of losing their husbands. They felt, time and time again, that their marriage was at stake.

However, when the women were asked, "Do your commitments to school interfere with your marriage and/or family relationships?" the majority of people answered, "no." Those who answered "yes" (47 percent) qualified their answers by stating that problems usually arose on weekends or at night when they needed to study and their families wanted their attention or they didn't feel as if they had enough time to keep the house as clean as they had previously. One woman mentioned, for example, that everything was "okay" as long as she did her school work after her "primary job" was finished. Many of the women felt this way about their commitments to their families:

> There's certain times when you have to decide what you're going to do especially on the weekends when my family would like to go do something and I've got a test coming up on Monday. I just can't do it . . . A lot of times it's intended that the mother is the thermostat, you know, she is kind of in charge. She's in charge of the ups and downs and whether things get done. I have taken myself out of that role every once in awhile because I don't have time to do it.

If there were problems caused by outside commitments, they were usually due to time constraints, but most of the women felt that school commitments did not interfere with their family commitments. Nevertheless, their husbands and children often had conflicting opinions on the matter.

This is interesting since over two-thirds of the women felt that their commitments to their family interfered with their school work. In other words, they felt that they were sacrificing themselves personally for their families. They felt that their primary commitments were to their families, that when someone was "sick" they would drop everything they were trying to accomplish to care for that person (if only temporarily), that they were pursuing school on a limited basis in comparison with their family commitment and that they might finish faster or go farther in school if they were not committed to family.

They relinquished personal satisfactions in order to meet family goals and they were sensitive to the needs of their husbands and children above their own needs. Nonetheless, families were often angry and threatened when it came to mother's pursuing outside goals. Likewise, many women perceived terrible risks associated with their decisions to go to college.

> I used to think, my God, I've been dead for fifteen years. And all of a sudden I woke up and said to myself, I'm not going to talk to the washer and dryer anymore. I swear I know that I have to do something for myself and that's the only way that I'm going to have sanity and I knew I couldn't stand it anymore, that I had to have something regardless of whether it broke up the marriage or not. I had to have it and I was willing to take that chance . . . Are you willing to take the chance that your marriage might fall apart and it might end? If you are, try it. If you aren't, if security means more to you, then you have to live by that. If you want it bad enough, you'll do it regardless.

This brings up two important questions. First, what did these women's husbands desire from the marital relationship that caused them to become upset when their wives entered the academic environment? Why were they threatened? Second, what kind of security is this woman talking about?

The first question cannot be answered by the data collected for this study. The question stands unanswered. The second question can be analyzed from a financial point of view.

Financial security was extremely important to these women. Leaving the marriage or being pushed out of the marriage could have very detrimental consequences in terms of standard of living for women who had most often worked as secretaries when they had worked. Many of their husbands were in the $30,000 and above bracket.

Family Income and Divorce   All of the women who were divorced in the sample experienced a drop in annual income as a result of the divorce. For three women the difference in total annual family income was not more than $5,000. But for the rest of the divorcees the difference was $10,000 or more. The difference in total family income before and after divorce ranged from a drop of a few thousand dollars to a drop of over $30,000 per annum. Most people experienced a loss of about $15,000 a year.

A loss as high as this forced them to alter their life styles tremendously, particularly because most of these divorcees did end up with custody of their children. Thus, they have few skills, their family income has dropped dramatically and they have approximately two children to support. The total scene for these women is somewhat distressing. School becomes, for them, a key to reestablishing a better standard of living.

The same situation applies to the widows who were interviewed. By and large, widowhood, for these women, correlated highly with financial problems. These people were in school to find a way to make a living wage.

The married women in the sample also worried about financial loss. They worried about what might become of them in the event of divorce. They spoke freely and openly about possibilities of divorce and what that might entail momentarily, and, from what the divorced women experienced, their concerns were well-founded.

Reentry women face barriers in their own families. They worry about money since they feel they have very few marketable skills. They worry that they are not spending enough time with their children and they feel that their husbands are not pleased with their involvements outside of the home. Still, there is one more concern which emerges as a problem in the women's immediate environment: old friends.

Change and Others:
The Case of Old Friends

When the women in this study were asked "How have your friends reacted to these changes in your life," a number of women paused and then asked, "Which friends, my old friends or my new friends?"

They claimed new friends were very supportive, as we shall see in the next chapter, but old friends had mixed reactions. Their attitudes ranged from support to the extent of going back to school themselves, to disapproval and outright shock.

Some women said that their friends were envious because they "were not in a position to do it themselves," some thought the women were "wasting their time," some were "jealous or puzzled as to what they would do with all that education." Some friends called the women "gutsy" or "crazy." They could not see the point of a family woman pursuing a college degree and they felt that they would never do it themselves. The most common reaction of old friends was the classic "And at your age?!"

For the most part, the reaction of old friends was indifferent or negative.

> They mostly are IBM wives also. They are very much ground up with things, material possessions, prestige of their husbands' jobs and what it does for them. They're pretty content with playing the social role and not working in careers or anything like that so they think I'm crazy. They think I gave up an awful lot. They don't understand my needs or why they should be needs because they think I had everything.

This woman was one of those whose marriage had dissolved and, for her, a desire to meet some of her own needs outside of the marriage had contributed to the causes of divorce. Many women felt that their old friends saw their new involvements as a threat. Often they were asked, "What do you want a degree for, what will you do with it?" One woman's sister "disowned" her with the statement, "How can you give up what you've got?" Another woman felt this way:

> I've found myself more interesting, not only for others but for myself . . . I haven't stayed in the same rut as my old friends. They can't understand my dedication to getting the degree and wanting to do something. They think I've gone off my rocker. My father thinks I'm crazy.

It appears as if the women's behavior was tolerated as long as school was a sort of "sideline" but once it became a major goal, some of the humor was dispensed with and the sanctions began to come down. Friendships changed, husbands and wives collided and children expressed disappointment.

In this chapter, we have observed that *women pursue outside interests only to the degree to which their involvements are comfortable for their family and others around them.* If they push their activities beyond this level, serious trouble is likely to arise in the microenvironment of the family. Women will often drop out when the familial pressures become too great even though it may be crucial to their mental and physical health to continue to pursue their activities.

To carry on in the face of adversity may be difficult and practically impossible for many reentry women. Pushing ahead might create a very risky situation and oftentimes a good deal of stamina is a prerequisite for action.

7
Rewards and Momentum

In spite of setbacks in the immediate environment, 75 percent of the women in this study were career-oriented and were motivated to complete a college degree. As we saw in chapter 5, these women were very much involved in making plans for the future and working toward their goals in a step by step manner. They sought satisfaction, a sense of purpose and the freedom to contribute to their families financially.

The rewards accrued by these women outweighed the costs associated with personal achievement. Benefits were manifest in many forms. The women perceived a positive, empathetic support structure operant in the school setting. Their attitudes toward others were increasingly positive. They had high grade point averages, which helped to increase their self-esteem. In addition, they felt that they would personally have an effect on society as a result of their studies and career pursuits.

A Matter of Emotional Support

In the beginning, entering school was not easy. For many women the Identity/Integrity Crisis became more complex as they entered the hallowed halls of academe. They did not "fit in." As they suffered through registration lines, their attitudes were ambivalent. They panicked in crowded bookstores at the beginning of the term. They could not find the classrooms that had been assigned to them. The campuses seemed to be filled with the young, glowing faces of "traditional" students whose whole lives seemed to stretch out before them like pathways of hope. The "kids" would have enough time to reflect and choose. The reengagement students felt pressured.

> When I first went, I was scared. I didn't know what I was getting into because I had been out of school for ten years . . . I was afraid. After ten years, I was older than most people in college. I was worried. You couldn't make me raise my hand to ask questions. Times when I didn't have a sitter, I took my two daughters to school with me. I'd backpack one and carry the other. It got to the point where the teachers didn't like it but it was the only way I could go to class.

Apprehension was the common feeling which characterized this era in women's lives: "I felt apprehensive, very desirous of the idea . . . [Apprehensive] because I might not be able to do it. I hadn't used my brain for a long time. It was very difficult. My concentration was very, very bad at the beginning." The question of whether or not they could discipline themselves to do the work arose often:

> It was worrisome because I'd forgotten whether I could discipline myself to read in a disciplined way. The first semester was just absolutely awful. It was horrible . . . You don't know what you can do and what you can't do and I felt miserable.

Although nearly all of the women reported similar feelings, for most that attitude changed after the initial entry and they began to gain self-confidence. However, a few never felt comfortable in the setting, even though they knew they had to stay there in order to reach their goals. These were the women who identified with and resented the term "retread," which was sometimes carelessly used in reference to reentry women. Nonetheless, these "out of place" women remained in the distinct minority.

The Opportunity for Social Contact   One study which assessed women's motivation for working found that women cited job-related factors, such as desire to work at something which provides interest and satisfaction for its own sake, and the opportunity for social contact. These reasons for returning to work were at least as important as economic ones (Cf.

Lansbury, 1977). This was particularly true for older women. Younger women were more likely to work out of economic necessity.

At the time of the interview, over two-thirds of the women in the present study had come to feel at ease in the academic setting and many attributed this to new opportunities for personal growth and social contact. Often, it was a "reengagement program" which drew women into the school and helped them to feel at home. One woman stated: "It's a very good program and I definitely feel that it's important to have because I think we all have fears when we come back to school for whatever reason." More concisely, another woman approached the question of comfort in the setting in the following way: "I feel very much a part of the setting [because of] the number of women who are in the program. I don't know if it was the actual program but it was as much the interaction with the students of the same age." In general, the longer the women had been "engaged" at their respective schools, the more psychological support they perceived. Some people perceived that they had made a conscious effort to become a part of the setting, like this woman: "I have chosen to become a part of this school. I feel you're always on the outside until you decide to step on the inside no matter what situation you're in." Less than one-fourth of the women "remained on the outside." Again, two-thirds of the women felt that they belonged in school. Some mentioned that they paid taxes which supported the school and therefore it was "their" school in a very literal sense. Thus most women who were threatened by the campus situation in the beginning rapidly overcame those feelings of insecurity.

Further, they began to make new friends. Thirty-two women believed they had acquired friends since they started school and most of these friendships involved women in the same position, thus they felt they were of a deeper quality than their previous friendships.

> I think there's a different quality to friendships now. Part of that is probably because I'm older but another really large factor in that is that when you are a housewife and are at home looking after small babies, the people that you have the most in common with are other people who have small babies and it's a transitory interest and so once you've outgrown that stage you may find yourself not having anything to talk about. Where it's a deep, gut-level interest that you have in common, the friendship tends to go deeper.

Women perceived their friendships to be more important because they perceived a "difference in their environment," and "a widened world view." They perceived a "broad range of resources" and an "extensive support system" which they had never experienced before. A few women saw their friendships as deeper because they were now in a situation where they could meet people apart from the "couples context" within which they had operated in the past. Most of the women felt that they were putting more energy and effort into their new friendships than they had in previous relationships and they felt that the result of that was a strong psychological support system.

Many women were inspired by the fact that this was the first time in their lives that they had their own friends apart from their husbands' occupational worlds: "Before I went to college, I only had my husband's friends who were my friends. Now I know a lot of people who know me, but don't know my husband." They felt that their husbands had always had private lives by virtue of their jobs. Having a private life became a symbol of dignity and integrity. As such, the Identity/Integrity Crisis was resolved in part through the establishment of an individual identity and independent friendships. The women became less dependent upon men and less in awe of their husbands' worlds. One woman went so far as to state:

> You see, the thing that I'd always believed all my life is all I had to do is find the right man and I would find that certain something that I was looking for and now I know beyond the shadow of a doubt that that's not true. You don't find yourself through another person. And, the other part of it was I wanted to find some kind of significant work which is why I went to school. I would like to work, not just at any old job, and I get very bored very quickly on jobs. So, I haven't found anything to do in life that I got very excited about . . . I finally just got burnt out looking for a husband. I said, this isn't working. I'm going to chuck this. This is for the birds, you know, I mean I spent my entire life looking for this man, this certain man, you know, the knight on the white horse. And I don't think there is one.

After passing through that crisis, she can optimistically claim: "I've seen some things by attending a women's college. I think I realize now that women can do a lot of things I didn't think they could do. I'm really proud of women."

Relationships with professors were also important in the psychological support structure described by these women. Thirty-six out of forty-five felt that they had special relationships with their teachers. They said that their teachers had taken a special interest in them. Professors were seen as peers, which was conducive to an atmosphere of support and mutual exchange. However, at least one woman remarked that her teachers, as her peers, saw her as a threat to them because of her age, her knowledge of life, and her knowledge of the subject matter. Whether the relationship was characterized as basically positive, which was the usual case, or basically negative, the women felt that their relationships with their professors were different from other students'. Different most often meant special and highly rewarding. Overall, women felt that these relationships were pillars of the general psychological support structure which was characteristic of the academic environment.

All in all, two-thirds of the women felt that there was an excellent psychological support structure for what they were trying to accomplish. The other third felt that there was no support or were not aware of any if it did exist. The intervening variable here appeared to be the type of school the women were attending.

Women at the community college perceived a good psychological support system almost unanimously. Women at the women's college were less sure of the psychological support system and women at the university were divided and ambiguous about their relationships with other reengagement students, professors, and the amount of support they were receiving in general.

Most women perceived deeper friendships and a good deal of support coming out of those friendships. This added momentum to their struggle for higher achievement and helped to raise their self-esteem. More support still was added upon receipt of report cards at the end of the term.

Grades and the Reengaging Woman

Whether the women perceived support for their efforts or not within the academic setting, they did not underestimate their performance. Interestingly, these findings do not coincide with the results of other investigators. Most studies concerning self-assessment of academic achievement find that girls and women tend to underestimate their performance (Cf. Thagaard, 1975; Deaux and Emswiller, 1974; Dweck and Gilliard, 1975; Nicholls, 1975).

Of the forty women who had established grade point averages, thirty-six reported that they felt that they were doing "very well" academically. In fact, the reported grade point average for these forty women was 3.75 (B+). Needless to say, this average contained a number of straight A (or 4.0) averages. Perhaps these women can offer a truer estimation of their own abilities because of age and life experience. As one woman said:

> Before, except with my close friends, I never talked about my work or my art or what I did. And I was very surprised . . . I became bold. I mean I actually said things, competent things. I think it's age. Here, I find myself volunteering. Being older must have something to do with it.

Further, the majority of women did not feel that they had to compete for these grades. Eighteen women found school to be somewhat or very competitive, but twenty-three found school not at all competitive.

Of the eighteen women who found school a competitive environment, eight felt that they were competing for grades and the others perceived varying sources of competition ranging from the attitudes of their professors to potential competition in the job market. Of the women who did not perceive a competitive atmosphere, most claimed that their major source of competition was only themselves. They strove to outdo themselves and to be as competent as possible. The main goal became to unleash "sleeping" potential. A few women recognized that they did not feel competitive because they were isolated in the environment. This woman characterized the dominant attitude: "Personally, I think there's a thing in me that wants to do well, but for myself. I don't think I'm competing with other people that much . . . I push myself but I don't see it as competing against someone." Another woman offers: "I think we make our own competition, I think the competition's with ourselves."

By and large, the women felt that they were excelling in a noncompetitive, supportive atmosphere in which they were involved in meaningful interchange with professors and students. Their lives took on added depth. Their friendships took on greater quality and equality.

Going to college was stimulating and provided a great deal of satisfaction. A third of the women mentioned feeling very, very excited about their involvements in academia and very proud of the work they had done.

Shapers of Society

It is not just the satisfaction that these women gain from the process of going to school that is important to them, but of equal or greater importance is the impact that they hope to have on society as a result of their educations and as a product of the total experience that school entails.

All but one of the forty-five women interviewed felt that they would have an important effect on their families.

As we saw in the last chapter, most of the women held a more positive attitude toward their husbands and children and they felt that their educations would influence and benefit family members. Many women felt that they were already influencing their children as the children became more interested in reading and in their school projects. There was more family participation in the children's school work. Nearly all of these women saw themselves as positive role models for their children in the sense that their educations had opened up new worlds for all of them.

> As far as having any effect on society, I think my education will have an effect on the society that my children — my children as a part of society, in giving them an interest in reading and an interest in the world, speaking well, my vocabulary. If they don't understand what I say they ask me what the word means and they learn.

Another woman states: "It will have an effect on my kids by the things that I've brought home to them that I've learned things about — anthropology — I've been able to help them with their work, math and science, even though I got a B in statistics." Finally, another woman sums it up this way:

> I definitely think that as a child gets older, the more stimulating the mother gets, the better it is for the kid. In a lot of ways I think it's been really neat to be getting my education during my son's formative years because I'm probably more stimulating now than I will be once I've gotten out of school and I'm working full-time. It's been a plus for him.

Nearly all the women felt that they would have an effect on society through their chosen careers. They felt that their educations in conjunction with their life experience would aid them in helping people. In fact, 50 percent of the career-oriented women were interested in going into the social sciences in order to accomplish this goal. "Since I'm planning to go into social work, I see myself as having an important impact on clients, and although the education is not a prerequisite for that, it certainly helps me be more effective with what I'm doing."

Twelve women sought to influence others through their art or their writing. Many women felt that they would make good teachers, not only of their own children, but of other people as well.

Thus, the women strove to "shape people's minds" through their endeavors. By sharing with each other and with other women, they could help to influence women's thinking. Thirteen percent of these women saw themselves as positive role models for other women. They felt that if they could do it, other women could do it as well. Many of their friends had also decided to go to school as a result of witnessing a firsthand involvement. Much satisfaction resulted from acting as a guide for other women:

> It seems like I have an effect on everyone I come in contact with. I did not expect that . . . It seems sometimes overwhelming. It seems like I'm always "on," plugged in. Part of it is that other women start drawing it out. I go back to school and they say, "How did you do? What are you doing? How are things? That's really neat," and, "What are you doing from there?" and it just seems . . . A lot of women are hungry for the information.

Many women believed in the "ripple effect" of education. They claimed that an individual's education affects all of the social interaction into which that individual enters.

> I think education makes it possible to have more of an effect on society. It's just like throwing rocks and pebbles and ripples and things. What I do affects a lot of other people and it enables you to take on things with more confidence. I never heard anyone say they were sorry they finished college but I heard a lot of people say they were sorry they hadn't. If you haven't you think maybe there's something there you don't know and if you've been there, you know.

The women felt that they could have an effect on society. They were supported in their efforts and they were doing well in school. Despite the barrage of deterrents faced by many of these women, they still insisted on seeking a new sense of identity and integrity through reengagement in higher education and they were accruing much satisfaction from the additional new role of student. It was important to them to take on this interest after the "transitory interest" of children had ceased to constitute a major concern.

The Identity/Integrity Crisis is a result of anticipating or experiencing the role loss which accompanies the Shrinking Circle Stage. The resolution of this crisis comes with a changing perception of self.

Reengagement and Self-Esteem

Forty-two out of forty-five women experienced increased levels of self-esteem upon taking on the outside involvement of becoming a student. As the momentum for making the transition began to snowball, the women's attitudes toward themselves became more positive. They had more self-respect and more self-confidence. They began to use the "75 percent" of themselves that "had gone to waste":

> I began to realize I had to do something for myself . . . I had this feeling that I had to get out of my house. I had these fantasies of getting in the car and driving down the road and never coming back. My kids were pulling away too . . . I began to realize that I was this incredibly unique woman and only 25 percent of me was being used.

Making the transition from housewife to student inspired new hopes which were the result of incorporating a new major life project into a situation where major roles had been lost:

> I had had years of extreme frustration and depression and not going anywhere and just hanging by fingernails to just emotionally stay on an even keel for the benefit of the children. So [when I entered school] everything was new. Everything was good . . . I was feeding everything that hadn't been fed for awhile. My whole life was undergoing a transition.

When the women were asked if becoming a student changed their attitudes toward themselves, their responses were markedly confident and assured. Some of the remarks that were made included the following:

> I'm more confident . . . unleashing my potential.

> I'm pleased with myself . . . made it to be a senior . . . didn't flunk out.

> I'm directing my own life for the first time.

> I feel better about my abilities and my mind. I'm more satisfied, more content. I recognize my intellectual merits and I find it easier to talk to people.

> I'm more independent and confident. I'm more intelligent and more aware. I like myself better and enjoy more.

> I feel autonomous and independent.

I'm not angry anymore, not frustrated.

I'm proud of myself. I did well. I have achieved something.

I'm much more aware of who I am outside of the mother role. I realize my strengths and I'm more self-confident.

I'm more self-confident. I have less awe of academia.

I see myself as more important. I have a better idea of my identity and capabilities.

I've gained confidence. I've begun to look inside myself and I see things clearly.

My self-esteem has increased tenfold. I no longer see myself as a girl but as an independent woman.

The list goes on and on. Eighteen people mentioned feeling more self-confident. Eleven mentioned feeling more autonomous, more independent or more self-directed.

Over one-half of the women were increasingly confident when it came to recognizing their intellectual merits or potential. These people often mentioned that they now felt self-assured in any company, regardless of how well-educated or "important" others might be. Several women claimed that "they didn't know how smart they were" until they started school. They gained an all-around better sense of their identities and an improved self-image.

A striking number of women mentioned the butterfly-from-the-cocoon analogy or spoke metaphorically of the "great oaks which from little acorns grow." They were striving toward the discovery of a new identity just as the breathtaking butterfly emerges from its silken envelope to begin anew:

I think the benefits are just unlimited. One big tremendous thing going back to school has done for me is it has lifted my mental attitude. I knew I was crying a lot at home before I even came to school and I got to the point where I was withdrawing . . . It has given me self-esteem and confidence in myself. It has also given me new friends.

Labelling and the Metamorphosis   Becoming an oak or a butterfly often entailed two components of "labelling," one related to the process of going to school and the other related to the product which would be the result of that involvement.

First, the process of going to school enabled the women to attach labels to themselves which were not related to their roles as housewives. They became "students," "scholars," and "intellectuals." With regard to their children and other housewives, they became "role models." They became "thinkers," "strivers," and "doers." Further, they found themselves to be "very bright," "very smart," "highly capable," and "ambitious." They were able to "put a name on something" which they felt had "been there all along" but which had been "vague," "out of focus" or "undefined." For many women this labelling process became a matter of "unleashing potential" in a very directed, step by step fashion.

The label could not be separated from the metamorphosis. The label, in and of itself, became an intrinsic component of a spiraling self-esteem. The process through which the label or definition was attached, that is, becoming educated through a formal educational system, became the medium for establishing a new adult identity. The support structure, in terms of friendships, relationships with teachers and relationships with classmates which were a result of the educational structure, the high grades and the process of learning how to solve problems creatively, were all part and parcel of creating a new identity.

The second part of the labelling process came with the product of the studies, the formal degree. Some women claimed that they had always been involved in artistic endeavors, but they could now call themselves Artists. Some women had loved business, but they could now call themselves Businesswomen. They were able to catalog the knowledge that they had gained through life experience and they were able to identify themselves with titles other than Wife or Mother:

I always thought I had something. For a long time I always thought I could be a fantastic mother and that's what I was geared for. I don't know why I thought that. I just always thought it. I had such a ball with the kids that I figured, yeah, you were right. My attitude about myself now is that I know that I can really do things that I've been told I couldn't other than being a wife and a mother. When it comes to different management skills, it was assumed that I couldn't possibly do that. I found and proved that I could and I can do some of it rather well. I'm pleased that I can do better than I thought I could. I never realized that. I apparently have some base abilities that I didn't know I had which has made me feel good. Or else maybe I'm just putting a name on something that I kind of knew was there. I didn't really know it was there because it didn't have a name. What I found out about myself when I went to school is that A and B always equalled C, which I knew from life experience, but I could not put a name to it. School helped acknowledge what I already knew, put titles on things, whatever it was that I needed.

The labels helped the women to view themselves as more "important" individuals in the world. They felt that their children regarded them as such as well. The children could now "name" what their mothers "did." The women felt that this was increasingly important as more and more mothers entered the work force. Not only did it add a new dimension to these mothers' identities, it added a dimension to the identities of their children. The women were "doing something the children could be proud of."

As we have seen, about half of the children responded positively to their mothers' involvements outside of the home. The mothers' attitudes toward children were almost unconditionally more positive than they had been before. They were more understanding and patient. This, in turn, added to their own self-esteem. They were proud of themselves for being better mothers than they had been before when they had felt imprisoned or trapped by their motherhood.

This attitude extended to their husbands as well. They were increasingly satisfied with their husbands and felt that their marriages could take on new dimensions. Unfortunately, as we saw in the last chapter, the husbands did not always see their wives' involvements outside of the family from this perspective. Nonetheless, the women were happier and more satisfied.

Happiness and Satisfaction in Reengaging Women

In response to the question, "In general, how satisfied would you say you are?", over 90 percent of the women answered that they were "very satisfied" or "somewhat satisfied." In response to the question, "In general, how happy would you say you are?", 93 percent of the women answered "very happy" or "somewhat happy." Very few people felt indifferent, unhappy or dissatisfied. Further, there did not appear to be any significant trend concerning happiness or satisfaction that could be related to life stages.

It appears that as self-esteem increases, satisfaction and happiness with life increase as well. On one level, at least, these women were reaching a "balance" between family, and personal growth and achievement, which brought about increased happiness and satisfaction.

The Advantages of Age

The women were happier and more satisfied than they had been before "reentry." They had more friends. They had special relationships with their teachers. They enjoyed their families more and their self-esteem was greater. They had discovered titles for themselves and labels for what they did. In addition, they felt their age would work for them in the job market as well as in the academic world. Maturity became an essential aspect of their new-found identities.

Not only did women feel bolder and more competent because of their age, but many also saw their age as an advantage in the pursuit of their chosen occupation. Twenty women, 71 percent of those who were career-oriented, felt that their age was an asset that would work in their favor in the job market. Reasons given for this judgement included an "increased amount of life experience in comparison with the competition," which was mentioned by nearly half of the women. Another major reason for increased competetence was that the women felt that they "had more confidence in their personalities than when they were younger." Women stated that they were now "not as inhibited," "highly motivated," "more self-confident," "mature in outlook" and so on. A few people mentioned that they had an advantage over younger women in that they would now have no interruptions in their careers due to pregnancies or caring for children. As one woman mentioned:

> I see myself as more important. I'm as important as anybody else. I think I have a lot more confidence and a better idea of who I am and what I'm capable of . . . I'm clear about what I want. I like the idea, too, that once I get out of school I won't have career interruptions because I'm pregnant.

In addition, some people claimed that age would not be an issue in the particular field they had chosen. In fact, age had been a primary consideration in choosing the fields they did.

However, some women did see their age as a disadvantage. They felt it was because they were getting a late start which would interfere with the amount of education they could hope to attain. Age would also interfere with retirement benefits. A few said that they would have to "settle for less" in a career than young people. For example, if they had once aspired to be a psychiatrist, they would now have to settle for being a counselor. Also cited as causes for concern by this group were "ageism" and the possibility that they would be discriminated against as women in the labor market.

Yet, every women who perceived her age as a disadvantage also found ways to work around that disadvantage effectively. Many stated that they would work on their self-image or self-concept by "feeling okay about themselves and their age," "maintaining a high energy level," or by thinking that perhaps they might enjoy working into their old age if they could not retire. Others thought that they would ignore their age altogether. Some women said that they would lessen the potential drawbacks of their age by emphasizing their life experience and personal characteristics to prospective employers or by choosing a field where they knew they would be in charge. Several women mentioned the possibility of creating their own jobs in areas such as tutoring, working in their husband's businesses, or building their own clienteles in fields such as real estate, investment, travel and so on.

If age was seen as neither advantage nor disadvantage, it was usually because the women felt that it would not interfere in their choice of

TABLE 7.1

STAGE IN LIFE CYCLE AND ATTITUDES TOWARD AGE

Attitude Toward Age

Stage	Advantage	Disadvantage	Both	Neither	Total
Expanding Circle	2(4.5%)	0	1 (2.3%)	1 (2.3%)	4 (9.1%)
Peak Stage & Full House Plateau	15(34.1%)	4 (9.1%)	3 (6.8%)	3 (6.8%)	25 (56.8%)
Shrinking Circle	0	3 (6.8%)	2 (4.5%)	2 (4.5%)	7 (15.9%)
Minimal Circle	3 (6.8%)	2 (4.5%)	0	3 (6.8%)	8 (18.2%)
Total	20 (45.5%)	9 (20.5%)	6 (13.6%)	9 (20.5%)	44 (100%)

career because "how far you get depends on your personal qualities regardless of age."

The perception of age as an advantage or disadvantage had no correlation with the woman's actual age or stage of family at the time of the interview. A summary of attitudes toward age and life stages is presented in Table 7.1. Regardless of life stage or actual age, the reengaging women tended to perceive their age as an advantage.

Reentry and Identification with a Feminist Perspective

It is interesting that in addition to increased levels of self-esteem and new highly confident attitudes, these women also experienced an increasing identification with the Women's Movement and stronger feminist attitudes.

This new respect for the work of other women also served to build their own self-esteem and added momentum to their struggle. Women "who had gone before" became role models for them and their attitudes toward "what women could do" or "what women were supposed to do" were undergoing dramatic changes.

Each women who was interviewed was given a survey concerning her attitudes toward women to complete at her leisure. This survey was part of the Shortform Attitudes Toward Feminism Scale developed by Royce Singleton and John Christiansen (1977). The questionnaire made statements such as, "Woman are basically more unpredictable than men," "A woman who refuses to bear children has failed in her duty to her husband," "A woman who refuses to give up her job to move with her husband would be to blame if the marriage broke up," and so on. The women selected an answer ranging from "Strongly Agree" to "Strongly Disagree."

Surprisingly, although the reentry women had been very traditional in their behavior up to this point in their lives, they scored highly feminist as a group on this scale. In other words, they strongly believed in alternative roles for women. For example, in previous tests, members of the feminist association, National Organization for Women (NOW), scored a high 91.3 on the "attitudes toward women" scale, whereas highly traditional teachers involved in Fascinating Womanhood scored a low, non-feminist 51.0. The reentry women in this study, as a group, scored an average of 88.7, highly feminist on the "attitude toward women" scale. No significant trends emerged related to age, life stage, or type of school attended which would differentiate the responses on this scale.

Thus, the women were rapidly becoming feminist in their outlooks and they perceived numerous rewards associated with their reentry. In their own minds, the benefits of reengaging far outweighed the costs. There was no contest.

In their new capacities, they saw themselves as important role models for other women. We have seen that these women felt "turned on" and "plugged in" and eager to dispense the information that they had gained. Indeed, they viewed themselves as a new generation of mothers who would shape society through shaping their children and pursuing careers.

The ideas ring positive and the woman are energized. But, what of the other side of the coin? What of the sexism and ageism which have been documented to exist in our society? What becomes of the notion of the two-person career? Who will provide these women with the type of support they need in order to synchronize their roles within and outside of the household? Is their pursuit merely an exercise in futility? There are questions which are addressed in the next chapter.

8
Back in the Mainstream?

Women who have made marriage and family their major adult life project espouse an attitude of commitment toward these roles which tends to upstage non-family-related involvements. In an investigation of women's priorities, Russell Lansbury (1977) found that family considerations typically weigh heavier in women's occupational decisions than work considerations. Thus, if women are to attain career-related goals, a certain amount of juggling family and external commitments is necessary. Women strive to synchronize roles in a way which fully takes into consideration familial goals as well as individual goals.

The unfortunate result of operating by this "contingency orientation" is that women usually remain in a position of marginality in their external involvements while experiencing dissonance in the microenvironment of their families. Regardless of how strongly they desire to achieve personal goals, this confounding set of circumstances may keep them out of the occupational mainstream. Further, if family contingencies are not enough to deflect women's determination, they will probably face discrimination in the labor market.

For women, this can add up to a seemingly no-win situation in which men are viewed as important financial anchors.

Another Look at Marriage and Money

As we saw in chapter 7, if a woman is married, she will probably have a higher total annual family income than if she is a divorced or widowed head of household. All of the married women in our sample stated that the primary source of income was their husband's job. Divorced and widowed women, across the board, reported a loss of income and a dramatically decreased standard of living with the loss of their husbands. No one reported an increased income or an increased standard of living after a divorce or after becoming a widow, regardless of what subsequent activities were undertaken.

By the same token, remarriage for divorcees or widows nearly always meant an increase in total annual family income. Thus, by attaching herself to a male, a woman could usually be assured of a higher standard of living for herself and her children.

Financial security was an extremely important aspect of the marriage bond for these women. This is illustrated by the fact that the difference per annum between marriage and living as a single parent was about $15,000.

When the marital relationship is threatened, women's livelihood becomes threatened. This puts many women in the uncomfortable position of feeling as though they must cater to their husband's needs or whims. For example, they are attuned to their husband's mood changes. They are ready to move whenever husbands' jobs so require. This type of behavior is viewed as contributing to familial goals. Behavior which enhances women's individual opportunities for growth in non-family-related matters may be viewed as selfish by husbands and wives as well. This further compounds the problems women face in their personal transition period.

Society's general ambivalence about women's roles adds to the problem. The women interviewed herein were not sure what they "should" do. On the one hand, they felt better about themselves when they pursued activities outside of their families. On the other hand, their activities seemed to disrupt the family system upon which they so depended for their livelihood. They were fully cognizant of the fact that they had been in and out of the labor force, and that when they had participated, it had usually been at less rewarding jobs. They stated that if they were forced to return to work, they did not want to reenter the job market as low status, low-paid clerical workers. Hence, the drive for higher education was often viewed as a preventative measure which would provide a base to fall back on in the case of an emergency, yet, the women knew that their chances of achieving success on the outside were greatest when they sought fields where age and sex would not emerge as inhibiting factors.

Valerie Kincade Oppenheimer (1973) examined some of these dilemmas from a historical perspective. She notes that, in preindustrial America, the productive work of men and women was generally carried on within the context of the family situation. This caused women to be economically dependent upon their family of orientation and then upon their husbands.

As industrialization increased, however, productive labor became increasingly removed from the home. Yet to take women out of their homes obviously threatened traditional family institutions. One way of combatting this quandry was to limit the outside work period of women to the years before marriage. By this method, the traditional family unit could be integrated into the increasingly complex industrial society.

These attitudes pervade our notions of woman's work today. As Oppenheimer states:

> Normative attitudes which support the employment of single women but discourage the employment of married women (except for the poor) may then be interpreted as representing a partial solution to the problem of integrating the family into the economic system of an industrial society. By choosing this solution, however, a society develops a dependence on female labor to perform certain types of tasks, and, in turn, work organizations come to integrate female workers into their structures in ways that would be difficult to achieve with male workers. In other words, the sex differentiation of roles is carried into the occupational world. (1973)

The argument then continues that unmarried women to perform these roles are in short supply as economic development continues. Thus, the next step in adaptation is to draw women into productive roles in the economy at various stages of the life cycle.

A rising demand for productive labor on the part of women has set in motion a transition in women's economic roles, and as women's participation has increased during the past twenty years, women have become more demanding in terms of the nature of the work they wish to undertake. Oppenheimer concludes by stating that:

> What was once good enough for an interim activity becomes less and less appealing as women's work roles expand. There should

be rising pressures among some women, then, to break out of the traditional female occupations into the male occupational world.

Reengaging women are caught, not only in a personal transition with regard to changing life roles, but a social transition, with regard to expanding economic roles. But, for these women, the family remains a major priority which greatly constricts the amount of work they can undertake and the timing of their labor force participation.

Further, although they are not quick to discuss it, they perceive a great deal of sex discrimination in the society at large. They are required to work outside of the family when they expected that their primary lifetime involvement would revolve around the family. They are asked to work when they will not be working within the same structure that their husbands are working in, that is, the two-person career model. They will have no back-up familial support system. It all becomes very confusing. Finally, they have not been able to pursue their careers in a step by step manner and, therefore, the problem of facing age discrimination assumes special importance.

Realism and the Perception of Sex Discrimination

Thirty-two out of forty-five women felt that they had been discriminated against because of their sex. Nineteen of these felt that they had been segregated on jobs, not hired, not promoted or had received inequal pay because of being female. Others felt that they had been forced to do "woman's work," such as running out for coffee or making coffee for others. They had had to put up with patronizing attitudes toward them and they had been criticized for being "too assertive." Sexual advances toward them on the job had been common. They had been asked personal questions concerning the planning of their families at job interviews and a few women had been fired because of pregnancy.

Only ten women did not think they had been discriminated against or they were not sure. Some of these felt that they probably would be discriminated against in the future as they sought after careers, and might have been in the past had they not retreated to the shelter of marriage and motherhood. These women had striven to protect themselves from discriminatory attitudes, by and large, by not participating.

In other words, all of the women interviewed, however traditional in their behavior, anticipated sex discrimination in the labor market. As mentioned above, facing discrimination was one factor which had restricted them to the family in the first place. Since husbands could make more money, it would be to the wives' advantages to help their husbands with their career pursuits.

Further, when they did work, they still did most of the housework, thus working outside the family could be compared to having two jobs, the job in the house usually reported as being "three quarter time" even when the women were working full-time.

Rather than not participating because they are only "learning about the labor market as they age," as suggested in Stolzenberg's and Waite's Learning Hypothesis presented in chapter 3, these women are being eminently realistic in actively choosing a major, lifetime involvement with marriage and family. And although they are highly aware of the personal rewards they could accrue from outside activities, they are also cognizant of the high costs of pursuing those individual job-related achievements. Their attitudes are starkly realistic when the position of women in the labor force is taken into account.

The Position of Women in the Labor Force

We have seen that, in the main, women work because they need the money. They also work for a sense of self-satisfaction, recognition for a job well done and so on. In addition, because the periods of childbearing and childrearing are now concentrated into a shorter period of the adult life cycle, women have more years to give to uninterrupted paid labor. They can now pursue work seriously and continuously.

Unfortunately, however, though women are entering the labor force in greater and greater numbers, most of them still occupy positions on the less prestigious rungs of the labor ladder. Almost 80 percent of the total force of clerical workers and nearly 100 percent of all private household workers are women.

Arlene Skolnick (1978) optimistically notes that women's participation in the labor market is on the upswing with women now comprising 40 percent of all professional and technical workers. Although this sounds promising, she neglects to mention that two-thirds of all women professional and technical workers are teachers, librarians, nurses and dieticians. In contrast, they are only 5 percent of lawyers, 9 percent of physicians, 4 percent of architects, 2 percent of engineers, 3 percent of dentists and the like. By comparison, women are 71 percent of elementary and secondary school teachers, 94 percent of nurses, dieticians and physical therapists, 79 percent of librarians, 70 percent of health technologists and so on.

In other words, even when women do become professionals, they are
segregated into the lower rungs of professionalism. Wilbert Moore (1970)
outlined a number of criteria which are prerequisites: a full-time occupation,
a commitment to a calling, a lengthy education, a service orientation and
a large degree of autonomy regulated only by a sense of responsibility
toward the clientele. The professional group must have a formalized
organization with which the profession may regulate itself and the number
of professionals involved in the field.

Women rarely attain positions that meet all of these criteria. If they
do become professionals, they will most likely find themselves in one of
five occupational categories, each of which is a female field. Over 80
percent of women workers are concentrated here. Is this any wonder
when we begin to examine the nature of the social structure within which
women are trying to operate?

As we saw in chapter 2, even college women intend to marry and
have children. Marriage and motherhood is perceived as the axis of the
adult lifetime involvement. Women orient themselves around families
and the commitment to family colors the amount and nature of outside
involvements that a woman is willing or able to incorporate into an already
busy adult life.

When the activities of the wife/mother role complex begin to slacken,
women can realistically consider adding alternative roles. At this point,
however, they find themselves in the position of not being able to effectively compete with their younger counterparts in the labor market.
The effects of age discrimination begin to set in.

Ageism and the Reengaging Woman, or: "Old Blondes Just Dye Away"

Alleen Pace Nilsen, in an article entitled, "Old Blondes Just Dye Away"
(1978), talks about how Americans tend to belittle women as they age
whereas the same attitudes do not apply to men. She states:

> We value men for their experience, wisdom and accomplishments.
> These increase with age. But what we value women for is their
> physical bodies — their sexuality and their ability to reproduce
> the species. Physical bodies deteriorate with age and so if this is
> primarily what a woman has been valued for, then understandably
> as she gets older her value decreases.

Simone de Beauvoir (1970) takes this argument further by stating that,
not only are women not valued in the same sense as men for their wisdom

and experience, but they are more likely to be discriminated against in the paid labor market because of their age.

> Employers dislike the idea of taking on elderly people . . . Elderly women suffer even more from this discrimination than men, although their expectation of life is greater. This, it may be added, is no new phenomenon. In 1900 a woman of forty-five or a man of fifty had the greatest difficulty in finding a job. In 1930, both in New York and the States in general, between twenty-five and forty per cent of firms only took on workers below a given age: in 1948, thirty-nine per cent were doing the same. (p. 338–9)

Even though age discrimination has been clearly documented, less than one-fourth of the reengaging women openly perceived their age as a disadvantage in their career pursuits. Still, most of the rest would choose female fields in which the competition would not be as severe. This would seem to indicate that women tacitly acknowledge the age discrimination problem. Very few of the women we interviewed sought to enter the paid labor force on a competitive basis in areas such as business.

Perhaps the reason these women did not perceive very much competition is that they felt themselves to be altogether marginal to the competitive arena.

Clearly, these reengaging women emerge once again as Horatia Algers. They have relegated themselves to fields consistent with the nurturant or expressive female role. They can struggle upward, in a feminine capacity, with the support of others. In this way they may "succeed" while continuing to orient their work around their family commitments.

At the same time, reengaging women tend to remove themselves from any potential issues of sexism or ageism through continuing to maintain their marginality.

Reengagement Programs:
The Pros and Cons

The Bright Promise of Reengaging   Reentering at the college level is an answer to the Identity/Integrity Crisis. It may be viewed as a method by which women resolve the dilemmas which result from the role loss inherent in the Shrinking Circle Stage.

Reengagement programs take special care of their older students. They generally include provisions which make the stages of reentry less difficult for reengaging women. They try to help them to overcome initial fears through special counseling sessions and courses designed specifically to meet the needs of reentry women.

These programs are usually seen as a way of integrating women who are anticipating an "empty nest" back into the "mainstream." The women are guided as gently as possible.

Personnel involved in these programs see themselves as humanitarian and service-oriented. As one brochure notes, the program staff recognizes the personal problems of reentry women. They know that these women are:

– entering the job market for the first time
– planning to enter college.
– undecided in their career goals.
– interested in changing careers.
– unsure of how to combine family and school or career.

By entering this program, many women can work toward resolution of these issues.

Another brochure states:

The "Women in Transition" program is designed to meet the needs of women who wish to return to formal education after an absence of some years. This program is designed with you, the woman, in mind. It combines individualized attention, by women, for women, with a warm supportive group environment. In the program, you are given an opportunity to explore and express your hopes, thoughts and feelings with other women, who, like you, are in transition.

These programs advertise themselves as providing a "safe" and "confidential" environment where women can examine and reevaluate their "value systems." They know that they can help to build their clients' self-esteem. One flyer provides testimonials to enforce this idea:

. . . through this program I have no doubt now that I can manage. The other women in my group helped me define my goals. I guess the biggest change in me is that now I feel there is no conflict between going to school and being a good mother . . .

The promise of these programs is beguiling to an ever increasing number of women in mid-life. There will be much "personal encouragement" and "sharing of resources." Further, many programs offer "specially trained" advising on "how to discover the hidden job market," vital knowledge for the reengaging woman.

Reentry programs take pride in the success of their students and provide special protection from the harsh nature of academe so that more and more women can become achieving alumnae:

Our program is growing steadily as it provides the adult woman (over 25) who wants to try (or try again) the challenge of college work. We are so proud of our students who attempt this venture into college courses and also of our alumnae who have met the challenge and established themselves as full-time students.

Whatever your aim [our program] can promise a new and different change of pace and could perhaps reveal exciting new dimenisons of yourself. The courses offered carry no prerequisites, have no entrance exams, and do not call for previous college experience. Each course can be used to satisfy a requirement, or as an elective, in the College of Arts and Sciences. The courses are duplicates of regular campus offerings; however, they are adapted for the woman who has had some life experiences.

Because the purpose of [our program] is to provide a comfortable entry for persons who feel they would like to try college courses, we attempt to eliminate or at least soften the problems usually encountered when attempting to accommodate a new life project. Therefore we provide the following special services:

I. Simplified Registration Procedure . . .
II. Deferred Payment . . .
III. A [program] Coordinator . . .
IV. Scholarships . . .
V. Library Tours . . .
VI. Special Non-Credit Courses

Reentry programs offer women an exclusive atmosphere in which they can expand their personal potential. They point the way to occupational opportunities. If women have been trained in particular areas in the past, they can update their knowledge through reengaging. Self-confidence and a self-assured demeanor as well as opportunities to learn about and prepare for the labor market are the promises of reengagement programs for mothers in mid-life.

For society-at-large, these programs offer one way to counter age stratification as well.

Lifelong Education as a Combatant of Age Stratification   Reentry programs are a component of a movement toward establishing lifelong education in the colleges. Continuing education offers adults better use of their leisure time in addition to occupational opportunity and re-training.

Ann Parelius (1975b) adds to this list the important latent benefit of these programs, "fundamental changes in the mesh between age strata on the one hand, and educational and economic institutions on the other." She claims that better systems of lifelong education will free people from the "lockstep" pattern of "completing" their schooling at a certain age. The common pattern of educational systems today only serves to define and differentiate age strata in society by adding to the institutionalization of the conceptualization of certain life-cycle stages, defining social strata by disseminating new knowledge, and by socializing age cohorts through this type of knowledge dissemination (Cf. Parelius, 1975b). The "student role" becomes an age-graded, age-linked role.

Instituting programs for reentry and continuing or lifelong education help to provide an "open-endedness of opportunity for upward social mobility." People are enabled to move in and out of the educational arena at will.

Parelius concludes by stating that as "age links between timing of education, employment and marriage are dissolved, new personal and familial strains will evolve." She hopes that a greater sexual equality in the division of labor will be the result.

The Cash Component: Money for the Schools   Aside from the humanitarian services provided by these programs, the schools can profit through incorporating this population. Encouraging the older set to enter college helps to balance out the problems which arose as the postwar baby boom generation began to pass beyond college age.

Everyone benefits all the way around. Teachers retain their jobs. Schools stay in business. The population increases its general knowledge. Women in mid-life are provided with opportunities to increase their knowledge, to learn about the job market, to build their self-confidence and to preserve their sanity.

In the Wake of the Mainstream?   Unfortunately, this coin has another side. Joy K. Rice (1975) identifies four major issues which are ramifications of a continuing education track for women. These are:

(1) a discontinuous versus a continuous education and employment pattern for women;

(2) Accomodation to prevailing social roles and norms versus change and conflict;

(3) a separatist versus a nonseparatist view of education for women; and

(4) the problem of a remedial versus preventive approach.

First of all, the very nature and goals of these programs suggest that discontinuity is a necessity in women's lives. Rice claims that the assumption of discontinuity "not only finds its way into research methods and conclusions but is also translated into applied prescriptions for counselors and advisors." Phasing in and phasing out of the mainstream is encouraged by these programs which often neglect to mention that women's formal education may be completely outdated and their knowledge obsolete by the time they reenter. In other words, it may take more than a "few brush-up courses" to revamp their skills. Further, women lose the seniority they need for promotions when they drop out of the labor market to become mothers. As if this were not enough, women tend to be concentrated in "nongrowth" or "traditional" fields, such as education, in which they are more likely to be hurt by a tightening economic situation. These factors add up to a competitive disadvantage for women who have been removed from the educational and occupational arenas even for a relatively short period of time (Cf. Rice, 1975).

Secondly, as we have seen, women tend to be the accommodating partners in marriage. Work roles and marital roles do not necessarily come into conflict when women adjust and compromise their goals in order to meet others' needs. Continuing education is also predicated on the notion of accommodation. Reentry programs offer women a "second chance" to "find themselves" and to "expand their potential" "after everyone else is educated and out of the nest and a spouse is secure in his job and financial status." (Cf. Rice, 1975)

Thirdly, continuing education keeps mothers apart. Reentry programs "duplicate" college courses, but "adapt" them to meet the special needs of the woman at mid-life. These programs are designed under the assumption that women have special needs as a result of the gap caused by a discontinuous involvement. With more women in the work force, however, for increasingly longer periods in their lives, perhaps these programs will become obsolete.

In sum, reentry programs can be characterized as being accomodative, remedial and separatist with an underlying philosophy of discontinuity.

They respond only to symptoms of a growing social problem and com-
pletely fail to address the roots of the malady. The crucial issues are thus
sidestepped.

False Promise and Great Hope   On the other hand, continuing education
can be viewed as a way of integrating women whose primary adult project
of raising children is coming to an end, back into the mainstream of
educational and occupational life. Protective programs, wherein women
can express themselves and build their self-confidence while "retraining"
are thereby offered. These programs reeducate and build character,
and some feel that they also help to reduce age stratification in society.
Further, they help to keep schools which are facing declining enrollments
in business. This is the great hope of continuing education. Social services
are provided in order to meet the needs of a specific clientele. This target
population has been trapped in a classical double bind in a changing
social and economic situation. Reentry appears to be a method of rising
above that bind. Reengagement programs bridge the gap between the
family and the occupational realm at a time when entering that arena
seems inevitable. It can be argued, however, that these programs *hold*
out false promises by perpetuating a social problem rather than pro-
viding a remedy, or at best, providing only a shortsighted one. They
perpetuate a discontinuous education and employment pattern for women
even though, in the long run, these women will be facing sex and age
discrimination in the labor market. The perpetuation of this broken
involvement keeps women in marginal positions. Further, the programs
uphold the status quo through accommodating rather than solving a
social problem.

If women are tracked in secondary school, as we saw in chapter 2,
women are also tracked and separated from men in the colleges at mid-life.
This separatist approach becomes a remedial approach.

While purporting to alleviate the marginal position of women at
mid-life, reengagement programs also act to perpetuate women's marginal
situation.

A Question of Power

A few women make it through the mid-life transition unscathed. These
are the Horatia Algers who others strive to emulate. These are the successful alumnae about which reengagement programs boast. But what
of the average woman, the housewife and mother?

She is divorced or widowed and struggling very hard to make a living for herself. Or, she is married and her husband is resentful of her involvements outside of the home. Thus, if she is not fighting an unsupportive social situation in the home environment, she is fighting an unsupportive social situation in the general external milieu. Either way, it is a major struggle. She lacks power in both arenas.

In both areas, she is confronting potentially severe economic sanctions. Divorce is costly and external opportunities are inequitable. She is facing ostracism in the home and discrimination in the labor market.

Relying on personal characteristics to insure success in mid-life without a full understanding of the social situation at hand renders as credible programs or outlooks which may be regarded as individualistic or token-istic. Where a few can succeed, the majority face numerous and frequently insurmountable barriers.

Women pay a high price for carrying out their socially prescribed roles as mothers and housewives. They lose the power to control their personal destinies and they become fatalistic in their outlooks toward motherhood and the tasks and roles which being a mother entails. While they are waiting for "their turn," a particular status quo is developing in the family system which they do not have the power to change. The costs may be too high.

If they forge ahead against the odds and pursue work in the paid labor force, the chances that they will be discriminated against on the basis of their sex or their age are high. Nonetheless, women seek personal satisfaction through goal-oriented pursuits outside of the familial environment.

In any case, women do not develop the mechanisms they need to accrue the power to control their own futures when they take on the primary adult lifetime involvement of becoming wives and mothers.

The question which remains is: Ultimately, given the social milieu in which we operate, what options are open to women?

Biology and Destiny Revisited   Becoming a mother is a turning point in women's adult lives. It is a goal to which most women aspire and most women expect to incur the role of mother even if they intend to pursue other goals as well. Yet, becoming a mother in contemporary America usually means that a woman will not be able to compete as effectively as her male counterparts in the labor force. The burden of childcare will generally fall into her hands. If she does not carry out the childcare herself, she must make arrangements to see that the children are provided for.

The time and effort involved in this, not to mention the disruption caused by the pregnancy and birth itself, can be a terrible drain on a woman's energy. Further, the problem may be compounded by a lack of geographical mobility due to marital constraints.

A final contingency of the marriage/mother role complex is the fact that birth control methods are not necessarily reliable. One-fourth of the children reared by the women in this study were initially unwanted. The role of primary caretaker of the children is highly demanding and time consuming.

Aside from the problem of unsupportive husbands, age discrimination, sex discrimination, programs which perpetuate a separatist approach, financial dependency and so on, becoming a mother, in and of itself, is enough to keep a woman in a marginal position in the educational and occupational realms of social life. And, at least 90 percent of all women in the United States can expect to become mothers regardless of their educational or occupational status or achievements.

9
Quandaries at Mid-Life

In American society, women perceive little choice with regard to the responsibilities they will incur in adult life. For most women the pursuit of a career, for example, is a second rung objective easily displaced or deferred in favor of the primary goals of marriage, childbearing and childrearing.

In a sense, biology would seem to dictate destiny for women, yet we are now living in a technological age where women have access to more effective methods of birth control which allow increased control over the processes of reproduction. The childbearing years are concentrated into a shorter period in the life cycle and women experience a longer "empty nest" period. Also, as a result of technology, women are now enjoying a longer lifespan.

Women are expected to participate in the paid labor force, yet their participation remains sporadic because of the inevitable childbearing function. Women are not able to compete effectively and they remain in the lower rungs of the labor force in marginal positions.

Thus, women's presence is demanded in two worlds. Full and active participation is still required in the home and women are in demand in the market place. Because women are at a competitive disadvantage in the labor market, they often question the nature of their status in that realm. Further, when the state of marriage appears to be unstable, women question their marital involvement. The result is that women are seeking involvement in the labor market as a form of self-preservation as well as for a sense of self-satisfaction. They are demanding a "fair" opportunity structure in work but they are not able to meet the demands of that world in the same sense that men are.

This can become a grave dilemma for women in mid-life, women who have borne all the children they intend to and can conceive of the termination of the mothering role as they have known it. Conflict may arise within individual women, in their family situations and in their external involvements.

This chapter summarizes some of the ideas which have been presented in the foregoing chapters and presents a framework through which we may view women's adult life cycle. We will reexamine how women are coerced into becoming mothers, how they adapt to that role and seek to accommodate that position, how conflict arises when the structure of that role undergoes change and how the transition out of that role takes place. Finally, we will examine the new affiliations women become involved in and the meaning of women's new affiliations.

Coercion

Women are mandated to become mothers through a complex interplay of religion, tradition, law and so on. In girls' "first encounters with their own futures," they learn that they will become mothers in adult life. Children are perceived as a logical extension of the marriage bond.

As the women in this study became wives, they accepted the "package deal" of marriage and motherhood. The event of marriage dramatically restructured women's daily activities, but the birth of the first child was even more significant. At that point, the women usually left the labor force and became full-time mothers. The children became the "crusade" for the mothers and being a mother provided a social identity complete with full-time routines and child-centered activities.

Adaptation

For women, the adult life cycle cannot be divided from the life cycle of the family. The events which influence the stages of the family are the same events which influence the stages of women's lives. Marriage, the birth of the first child, the completion of childbearing, the children entering school, the first child leaving home, the last child leaving home, the empty nest period and the loss of a spouse are all occurrences around which women design their activities.

At age twenty-one, most of the women in the present sample were married. Upon marrying, they adapted their activities to meet the demands of their husbands' school or work involvements. For many this meant relocating immediately which often required that they leave jobs, friends, family and other familiar circumstances. Many women felt that there was a gap in their lives that marriage alone could not fill. It was a sensation of loneliness or lack of fulfillment and children were often conceived to fill that space.

By age twenty-three-and-one-half, most of these women had given birth to their first child. At that time, their primary activities were maintaining the household and taking care of the children. Internal pressures began to arise at this time. Many women felt that they had not been adequately "trained" for the mother role. On-the-job training, where immediate performance was required, was difficult. Further, the women spent these early adult years sporadically moving in and out of the labor force as their family financial situation demanded. They were frustrated by this type of marginal involvement.

In most cases, the women had completed their childbearing at about age twenty-eight. By this time, the women were organizing their lives entirely around their families. They had adapted to the role of being the flexible partner in the marriage and the "thermostat" of the family.

Accommodation

Because of the tremendous responsibilities involved in mothering on a day to day basis, most of the mothers "took each day as it came" rather than trying to plan for the future. When planning for the future was done, it was usually for their husbands' future or for the future of the family as a unit. Their husband's future was his occupational future. The future of the family revolved around his job. The women were so involved in the future of the family and the future of their husbands' jobs that, for themselves, they were forced to adopt a day-by-day accommodative style. The mothers had to accommodate their families, to develop a contingency orientation, in order for the family to meet its collective goals.

As the family moved through its consecutive stages, the women began to engage in anticipatory socialization as they perceived the onset of the Shrinking Circle Stage. At this point, they began to conceptualize the course of their individual futures with regard to goals external to the family. They knew that they would have to take on other involvements to compensate for the imminent role loss which they felt they would be facing. They put themselves in a position to learn more about the labor market.

The problem which arose at this time was that, during the time they had been accommodating their families with a day by day flexible orientation, a certain status quo had been developing in the family situation. Husbands and children had become dependent upon the woman's accommodative behavior. The family system had been enabled to function in a specific way because of the mother's contingency orientation. Hence, any changes which might ensue could be seen as a threat to the familial status quo.

Conflict

Conflict became more predominant in the family as women began to alter their accommodative patterns. However, this trend toward change was a direct result of the personal conflicts these women were experiencing with the perception of alterations in the structure of the wife/mother role.

In retrospect, two-thirds of the women felt ambivalent about the choices they had made concerning motherhood during early adulthood. The "package deal" of marriage and motherhood became a less fulfilling activity as they moved through the life cycle. There were three reasons for this. First, they found themselves wanting to be "distinguished" from other mothers and recognized for their own individual accomplishments. Second, they perceived that the mother role could be conceived of, in part, as a custodial role of temporal duration which would be coming to an end. Third, they were often facing an economic need which forced them to consider participation in the labor market. They anticipated being a single head of household, or they found themselves in that position, and they wanted to try to maintain the standard of living which they had known.

Experiencing the role conflict, which resulted from disappointment in, or termination of, the mother role, often led these women to re-evaluate their priorities and to consider involving themselves in productive situations outside of the family. In other words, they often began to consider alternatives relevant to their own personal achievements apart from the family. However, in order to act upon their thoughts, they needed to perceive that they had the resources to do so. They had to have a faith in the reasonableness of what they thought they might achieve and they had to have a strong desire for the pay-off which entailed the ability to think through the costs and benefits inherent in their plans. Most of the time, these women found themselves in a crisis situation before they could confront change. The crisis was induced by structural alterations of the mother role.

The perception of a crisis period usually meant that the mother role was carefully reevaluated. One-third of the women wished that they had had fewer children in retrospect. In addition, these women conceded that one quarter of the children that they had borne and raised had been unwanted initially, yet they had seen it as their personal destiny to raise these children.

Women are not the only ones experiencing role conflict at this time. Their husbands begin to experience contradictions in their status when wives take on outside involvements. As the women became more outward-oriented and their behavior became more goal-directed, husbands felt threatened and became resentful. As wives became less accommodative, husbands experienced more life stress.

Nonetheless, wives were more satisfied with their marriages when they pursued activities unrelated to their families. In fact, they were much more satisfied with life in general.

Transition

As women experience increased levels of social contact, after having been somewhat isolated in the wife/mother role, they experience "validation of self" and increased levels of self-esteem. They feel more independent, more self-confident and less in awe of the world outside of their families.

Furthermore, they gain a "healthy respect" for other women and identify themselves as feminist-oriented. Reengagement becomes the framework within which women feel more intellectually competent, autonomous and self-directed.

This is a marked contrast to the self-concept these women held when their identities were based on the perception of themselves as wives and mothers. Becoming a student provides women with a new dimension of activity. Reentering entails developing an alternative identity structure in keeping with the new routines incorporated into everyday life.

Wives and mothers in mid-life feel more powerful and comfortable with themselves as they extend their involvement beyond the family system. Whether they are actually more "powerful" is another issue.

The Meaning of New Affiliations

We have seen that women depend upon marriage in order to attain a desired standard of living. Becoming a wife usually means enjoying a higher income. Further, women are aware of sex discrimination in the labor market and they know that, if they work, their physical needs will not be met by others. And they will still be doing most of the household maintenance.

The women in this study helped their husbands to achieve. During early marriage they felt that their husbands' accomplishments were also their own accomplishments. They had bonded with their husbands as a method of self-preservation and they saw the creation and perpetuation of a family system as the most important and realistic goal of their early adult life.

At the time, phasing in and out of the labor market, as familial need dictated, seemed logical. In fact, the women perceived little choice with regard to this matter or in becoming wives and mothers. Yet they perceived this segment of the adult life cycle to be temporally limited, and, with the birth of the last child, they began to make plans for their personal futures.

Unfortunately, they discovered that they had "paid a high price" for carrying out their socially prescribed roles in the manner in which they had been dictated. They felt that they had lost control over their personal destinies and they had become fatalistic in their outlooks toward motherhood. A status quo had developed in the family systems they had created, which they often felt they did not have the power to alter. While husbands, with their wives' support, had developed mechanisms to accrue the power to control their personal destinies, year by year, the women relinquished control over their independent futures.

Reentry offered new hope and a new identity. However, the experience was usually rife with new problems as well. First, the women realized that, because of the time and effort involved in childcare along with the lack of geographical mobility, competitive participation in the labor market had been precluded. They had not been able to pursue personal goals in a systematic way. Secondly, they discovered that their families were largely unsupportive of their involvement in academe. Thirdly, they still faced age and sex discrimination in the labor market.

Since no alternatives were readily available, the women tried to work around these problems. They remained optimistic and determined despite the numerous barriers inhibiting their personal struggle for higher achievement. The women were proud of their accomplishments in the home, they were proud of the children which they had lovingly nurtured and they were proud of the sacrifices they had made for their families. Finally, they were facing the future, however uncertain it might seem, with dignity.

Areas for Further Study

Many issues have been raised by this study. Of these, the following areas are critical:

1. The "contingency orientation" has been utilized to explain women's accommodative behavior. I would like to add a further dimension to this concept by pointing out that traditional women experience a strong "mid-life drive for money and meaning." They reevaluate their relationships and activities which results in a goal-directed future orientation. Therefore, the "contingency orientation" appears to be a temporary outlook. Women expect to "accommodate" for a finite period. Accommodation is seen as appropriate only in certain segments of the adult life cycle.

2. At the time the "contingency orientation" no longer seems appropriate, "biographical rupture" will take place. Women will find themselves facing a crisis situation. This will occur when the structure of the wife/mother role is changing in such a way that women experience a lack of consistency in what is expected of them and in what they expect for and of themselves. At this time, women will no longer be able to conceive of the wife/mother role as the exclusive reality.

3. In examining women's labor force participation, it would be helpful to take into account the Temporality Hypothesis. In addition to marriage and fertility plans and early marital fertility behavior, we need to explore women's mid-life involvement in the educational and occupational arenas. This will aid in understanding the status attainment process for women and could provide the groundwork for establishing policy in education and employment.

4. Women in mid-life seem to fall victim to the Horatia Alger Syndrome. They tend to choose fields wherein their age and circumstances will not have a direct bearing. They rely on sponsors in order to achieve. This approach has been referred to as individualistic and tokenistic. It is, however, realistic. Women are blamed for espousing this orientation when they are, in fact, the victims of a specific set of changing social and economic circumstances.

5. Reengagement programs may lack the sophistication required to begin to alleviate the quandaries of mid-life presented herein. The programs may be perpetuating the problems they are purporting to solve by maintaining a separatist approach. Further,

I find the terminology objectionable. Women at mid-life have been engaged in fulfilling, what they perceive as, their social obligations. Careful evaluation of these programs is in order.

Only through acquiring an in depth understanding of each of these areas can we begin to work toward altering the circumstances which preclude women's effective competition and keep women from achieving to the degree to which they are capable. Only through understanding these areas will we be able to understand the quandaries of mothers in mid-life and the social framework within which they are struggling to make a transition from one occupation to another.

References

Bernard, Jessie. *The Future of Marriage*. New York: World, 1972; Bantam, 1973.

———. *Women, Wives, Mothers*. Chicago: Aldine, 1975.

———. *The Female World*. New York: The Free Press, 1981.

Chickering, Arthur W. and Robert Havighurst, "The Life Cycle." In Arthur W. Chickering and Associates, *The Modern American College*. San Francisco: Jossey-Bass, 1981.

Katz, Joseph. "Home Life of Women in Continuing Education." In Helen S. Astin, editor, *Some Action of Her Own*. Lexington, Mass.: Lexington Books, 1976.

Smith, Ralph, ed. *The Subtle Revolution*. Washington, D.C.: The Urban Institute, 1979.

Bibliography

Alexander, Karl L., and Bruce K. Eckland. "Sex Differences in the Educational Attainment Process." *American Sociological Review,* 5 October 1974, 669–682.

Almquist, E., and S. Angrist. "Career Salience and Atypicality of Occupational Choice Among College Women." *Journal of Marriage and the Family* 32 (1970): 242–49.

Almquist, E., and S. Angrist. "Role Model Influence on College Women's Career Aspirations." *Merrill-Palmer Quarterly* 17 (1971).

Alsbrook, Larry, "Marital Communication and Sexism." *Social Casework* 57 (1976): 517–522.

Angrist, S. and E. M. Almquist. *Careers and Contingencies; How College Women Juggle with Gender.* New York and London: Dunellen, 1975.

Atchley, Robert C. *The Social Forces in Later Life: An Introduction to Social Gerontology.* Wadsworth Publishing Company, 1972.

Bacon, Carolyn, and Richard M. Lerner. "Effects of Maternal Employment Status on Development of Vocational-Role Perception in Females." *Journal of Genetic Psychology* 126 (1975): 187–193.

Bell, Carolyn Shaw. "Age, Sex, Marriage, and Jobs." *Public Interest* 30 (1973): 76–87.

Berger, Peter L., and Thomas Luckman. *The Social Construction of Reality: A Treatise in the Sociology of Knowledge.* Anchor Books, 1976.

Bernard, Jessie. *The Future of Motherhood.* New York: Penguin, 1974.

Beyer, Mary Alice, and Robert N. Whitehurst. "Value Changes with Length of Marriage: Some Correlates of Consonance and Dissonance." *International Journal of Sociology of the Family* 6 (1976): 109–120.

Brennan, Angelica F. "Some Shifts in Psychological Stresses Reported by Re-entry Women in Education." Capitol Campus, Penn. State University, May 27, 1979.

Burke, Ronald J., and Tamara Weir. "Relationship of Wives' Employment Status to Husband, Wife and Pair Satisfaction and Performance." *Journal of Marriage and the Family* 38 (1976): 279–287.

Chamberlain, Audrey, "Planning vs. Fatalism." *Journal of Biosocial Science* 8 (1976): 1–16.

Condry, John, and Sharon Dyer. "Fear of Success: Attribution of Cause to the Victim." *Journal of Social Issues* 32 (1976): 63–85.

Cummings, Laurie Davidson. "Value Stretch in Definitions of Careers Among College Women: Horatia Alger as Feminist Model." *Social Problems* 25 (1977): 65–74.

Darian, Jean C. "Factors Influencing the Rising Labor Force Participation Rates of Married Women with Pre-School Children." *Social Science Quarterly* 56 (1976): 614–630.

Deaux, K., and T. Emswiller. "Explanations of Successful Performance on Sex-Linked Tasks: What's Skill for the Male is Luck for the Female." *Journal of Personality and Social Psychology* 29 (1974): 80–85.

de Beauvoir, Simone. *The Coming of Age.* Warner Paperback Library, 1973.

Dellas, Marie, and Eugene L. Gaier. "The Self and Adolescent Identity in Women: Options and Implications." *Adolescence* 10 (1975): 399–407.

Diamond, Irma. "The Liberation of Women in a Full Employment Society." *The Annals of the American Academy of Political and Social Sciences* 418 (March 1975): 138–146.

Doherty, Edmund, and Cathryn Culver. "Sex-Role Identification, Ability and Achievement among High School Girls." *Sociology of Education* 41 (1976): 1–3.

Douvan, Elizabeth. "The Role of Models in Women's Professional Development." *Psychology of Women Quarterly* 1 (1976): 5–20.

Dowdall, Jean A. "Structural and Attitudinal Factors Associated with Female Labor Force Participation." *Social Science Quarterly* 55 (1974): 111–120.

Drummond, Hugh. "Diagnosing Marriage: Dr. D. says it's Terminal." *Mother Jones,* July 1979, 14–21.

Duncan, R. Paul, and Carolyn Cummings Perrucci. "Dual Occupation Families and Migration." *American Sociological Review* 41 (1976): 252–261.

Dweck, C. S., and D. Gilliard. "Expectancy Statements as Determinants of Reactions to Failure: Sex Differences in Persistence and Expectancy Change." *Journal of Personality and Social Psychology* 32 (1975): 1077–1084.

Elder, Glen H., Jr., and Richard C. Rockwell. "Marital Timing in Women's Life Patterns." *Journal of Family History* 1 (1976): 34–53.

Englander-Golden, Paula, "Differences in Attitudinal and Behavioral Feminism in Sex Role Stereotypes." Presented at the 22nd Annual Western Social Science Association Conference, April 1980.

Epstein, Cynthia Fuches. "Bringing Women In: Rewards, Punishment and the Structure of Achievement." *Women and Success: The Anatomy of Achievement.* Edited by Ruth B. Kundsin. New York: William Morrow and Company, 1974.

Etaugh, C. "Effect of Maternal Employment on Children: A Review of Recent Research." *Merrill Palmer Quarterly* 20 (1974): 71–97.

Eyde, L. D. "Eliminating Barriers to Career Development in Women." *Personnel and Guidance Journal* 49 (1970): 24–29.

Falk, William W., and Arthur G. Cosby. "Women and the Status Attainment Process." *Social Science Quarterly* 56 (1975): 307–314.

Farley, Jennie. "Coeducation and College Women." *The Cornell Journal of Social Relations* 9 (1973): 87–97.

Feldman, Saul D. "Impediment or Stimulant? Marital Status and Graduate Education." *American Journal of Sociology* 78 (1973): 982–994.

Felson, Marcus, and David Knoke. "Social Status and the Married Woman." *Journal of Marriage and the Family* 36 (1974): 516–521.

Ferber, Marianne Abeles, and Joan Althaus Huber. "Sex of Student and Instructor: A Study of Student Bias." *American Journal of Sociology* 80 (1975): 949–963.

Fichter, Joseph H. "Marriage and Motherhood of Black Women Graduates." *Woman in a Man-Made World.* Edited by Nona Glazer-Malbin and Helen Youngelson Waehrer. New York: Rand-McNally, 1972.

Franzwa, Helen H. "Working Women in Fact and Fiction." *Journal of Communication* 24 (1974): 104–109.

Fredrickson, Charles G. "Life Stress and Marital Conflicts: A Pilot Study." *Journal of Marriage and Family Counseling* 3 (1977): 41–47.

Gentzler, Rie. "PROBE: Toward Meeting the Needs of the Reentry Woman." Project Associate, PROBE, Harrisburg, PA, Pennsylvania State University, Capitol Campus, Middletown, PA, 1979.

Glick, Paul C. "Updating the Life Cycle of the Family." *Journal of Marriage and the Family* 39 (1976): 5–13.

Gysberg, N. C., J. A. Johnston, and T. Gust. "Characteristics of Homemakers and Career Oriented Women." *Journal of Counseling Psychology* 15 (1968): 541–46.

Hall, Douglas T. "Pressures from Work, Self, and Home in the Life of Married Women." *Journal of Vocational Behavior* 6 (1975): 121–132.

Hoffman, Lois Wladis. "The Employment of Women, Education and Fertility." *Merrill-Palmer Quarterly* 20 (1974): 99–119.

Hoffman, L. W. "The Value of Children to Parents." *Psychological Perspectives on Population.* New York: Basic Books, 1973.

Hoffman, L. W., and F. Nye. *The Employed Mother and the Family.* San Francisco: Jossey Bass, 1974.

Holstrom, Engin I., and Robert W. Holmstom. "The Plight of the Woman Doctoral Student." *American Educational Research Journal* 11 (1974): 1–17.

Horner, Matina. "Toward an Understanding of Achievement-Related Conflicts in Women." *The Journal of Social Issues* 28 (1972): 157–175.

Houseknecht, Sharon K. "Reference Group Support for Voluntary Childlessness: Evidence for Conformity." *Journal of Marriage and the Family* 39 (1977): 285–292.

Hout, Michael, and William R. Morgan. "Race and Sex Variations in Causes of Expected Attainments of High School Seniors." *American Journal of Sociology* 2 (September): 364–394.

Hunt, Janet G., and Larry L. Hunt. "Dilemmas and Contradiction of Status: The Case of the Dual Career Family." *Social Problems* 24 (1977): 407–416.

Hutchinson, Enid. "Fresh Horizons in Education and Employment for Women." *Society and Leisure* 6 (1974): 53–67.

Jaffe, Lorna. "Women's Place in Academe." *The Midwest Quarterly* 15 (1973): 16–30.

Jorgenson, David F. "The Effects of Social Position, and Wife/Mother Employment on Family Leisure-Time: A Study of Fathers." *International Journal of Sociology of the Family* 7 (1977): 197–208.

Kierfert, R. M., and G. I. J. Dixon. "A Preliminary Study of the Childless Couple." *Rocky Mountain Social Science Journal* 5 (1968): 119–28.

Kinnane, J. F., and Bannon, M. M. "Perceived Parental Influence and Work-Value Orientation." *Personnel and Guidance Journal* 43 (1964): 273–79.

Kirschner, Betty Frankle. "Introducing Students to Women's Place in Society." *American Journal of Sociology* 78 (1973): 1051–1054.

Klemmack, David L., and John N. Edwards. "Women's Acquisition of Stereotyped Occupational Aspirations." *Sociology and Social Research* 54 (1973): 510–525.

Kundsin, Ruth B. (ed.), *Women and Success: The Anatomy of Achievement.* New York: William Morrow and Company, 1974.

Lansbury, Russell. "Women and Work: An Attitudinal Study." *Australian Journal of Social Issues* 12 (1977): 112–119.

Lave, Judith and Shirley S. Angrist. "Factors Affecting Child Care Expenditures of Working Mothers." Working paper, School of Urban and Public Affairs, Carnegie-Mellon University, Pittsburgh, Pennsylvania, 1974.

Letchworth, George E. "Women Who Return to College: An Identity-Integrity Approach." *Journal of College Student Personnel*, March 1970, 103–106.

Levine, Adeline, and Janice Crumrine. "Women and the Fear of Success: A Problem in Replication." *American Journal of Sociology* 80 (1975): 964–974.

Levitt, E. S. "Vocational Development of Professional Women: A Review." *Journal of Vocational Behavior* 1 (1971): 375–385.

Lipman-Blumen, J. "How Ideology Shapes Women's Lives." *Scientific American* 226 (1972): 34–42.

Lopata, Helena. *Occupation: Housewife.* New York: Oxford University Press, 1971.

Maccoby, E. E. "Sex Difference in Intellectual Functioning," *Readings on the Psychology of Women.* Edited by J. Bardwick. New York: Harper and Row, 1972.

Mackie, Marlene. "Student's Perceptions of Female Professors." *Journal of Vocational Behavior* 8 (1976): 337–348.

Mayes, Bea. "Women, Equality and the Public High School." *Education* 97 (1977): 330–335.

Mitchell, Juliet. *Women's Estate.* New York: Vintage Books, 1973.

Moore, Wilbert. *The Professions: Roles and Rules.* New York: Russell Sage Foundation, 1970.

Nicholls, J. "Causal Attributions and Other Achievement Related Cognitions: Effects on Task, Outcome, Attainment, Value and Sex." *Journal of Personality and Social Psychology* 31 (1975): 379–389.

Nilsen, Alleen Pace. "Old Blondes Just Dye Away: Relationships Between Sexism and Ageism." *Language Arts* 55 (1978): 175–179.

Oakley, Ann. *The Sociology of Housework.* New York: Pantheon Books, 1974.

Oliver, Laurel W. "The Relationship of Parental Attitudes and Parental Identification to Career and Homemaking Orientation in College Women." *Journal of Vocational Behavior* 1 (1975): 1–12.

Oppenheimer, Valerie Kincade. "Demographic Influence of Female Employment and the Status of Women." *American Journal of Sociology* 78 (1973): 946–961.

Papenek, Hanna. "Men, Women and Work: Reflections on the Two-Person Career." *American Journal of Sociology* 78 (1973): 852–872.

Parelius, Ann P. "Change and Stability in College Women's Orientations Toward Education, Family and Work." *Social Problems* 22 (1975): 420–432.

Parelius, Ann P. "Emerging Sex-Role Attitudes, Expectations and Strains Among College Women." *Journal of Marriage and the Family* 37 (1975a): 146–153.

Parelius, Ann P. "Lifelong Education and Age Stratification: Some Unexplored Relationships." *American Behavioral Scientist* 19 (1975b): 206–223.

Peterson, Candida, and James Peterson. "Issues Concerning Collaborating Careers." *Journal of Vocational Behavior* 7 (1975): 173–180.

Press, J. M., and F. Whitney. "Achievement Syndrome in Women: Vicarious or Conflict Ridden." Mimeographed, presented at the Eastern Sociological Society, New York, 1971.

Rice, Joy K. "Continuing Education for Women, 1960–1975: A Critical Appraisal." *Education Record* 56 (1975): 240–249.

Rich, Adrienne. *Of Woman Born.* New York: Bantam, 1976.

Ritchey, P. Neal, and C. Shannon Stokes. "Correlates of Childlessness and Expectations to Remain Childless: U. S. 1967." *Social Forces* 52 (1974): 349-356.

Roby, Pamela Ann. "Toward Full Equality: More Job Education for Women." *School Review* 84 (1976): 181-211.

Roby, Pamela. "Women and American Higher Education." *Annals of the American Academy of Political and Social Science* 404 (1972): 118-139.

Rockwell, Richard C. "Historical Trends and Variations in Educational Homogamy." *Journal of Marriage and the Family* 38 (1976): 83-95.

Rosen, Bernard, and Carol S. Aneshensel. "The Chameleon Syndrome: A Social Psychological Dimension of the Female Sex Role." *Journal of Marriage and the Family* 38 (1976): 605-617.

Rubin, Lillian B. *Women of a Certain Age: The Midlife Search for Self.* New York: Harper and Row, 1979.

Russo, Nancy Felipe. "The Motherhood Mandate." *Journal of Social Issues* 32 (1976): 143-153.

Sawhill, Isabel U. "Economic Perspectives on the Family." *Daedalus* 106 (1977): 115-125.

Scanzoni, John. "Gender Roles and the Process of Fertility Control." *Journal of Marriage and the Family* 38 (1976): 677-691.

Schmelz, Jerome. "Rising Aspirations of American Women and the Declining Birth Rate." *International Journal of Sociology of the Family* 6 (1976): 179-196.

Schuck, Victoria. "Sexism and Scholarship: A Brief Overview of Women, Academia, and the Disciplines." *Social Science Quarterly* 55 (1974): 563-585.

Schwartz, Lita Linzer. "Women: Re-Entry and Challenge." *Journal of Sociology and Social Welfare* 4 (1977): 845-849.

Szinovacz, Maximiliane E. "Role Allocation, Family Structure and Female Employment." *Journal of Marriage and the Family* 39 (1977): 781-791.

Sewell, W. H., A. O. Haller, and A. Poites. "The Early Educational and Early Occupational Status Attainment Process." *American Sociological Review* 34 (1969): 82-92.

Simpson, Richard L. "Sex Stereotypes of Secondary School Teaching Subjects: Male and Female Status Gains and Losses." *Sociology of Education* 47 (1974): 388-398.

Singleton, Royce, Jr., and John B. Christianson. "The Construct Validation of a Short Form Attitudes Toward Feminism Scale." *Sociology and Social Research* 61 (1977): 294–303.

Skolnick, Arlene. *The Intimate Environment: Exploring Marriage and the Family.* Boston: Little, Brown and Co., 1978.

Slater, Philip. *The Pursuit of Loneliness: American Culture at the Breaking Point.* Boston: Beacon Press, 1970.

Smith, Eliot R., Myra Marx Ferree, and Frederick D. Miller. "A Short Scale of Attitudes Toward Feminism." *Representative Research in Social Psychology* 6 (1975): 51–56.

Solmon, Lewis C. "Women in Doctoral Education, Clues and Puzzles Regarding Institutional Discrimination." *Research in Higher Education* 1 (1973): 299–332.

Stolzenberg, Ross M., and Linda J. Waite. "Age, Fertility Expectations and Plans for Employment." *American Sociological Review* 42 (1977): 769–783.

Stroup, A. *Marriage and Family: A Developmental Approach.* New York: Appleton-Century-Crofts, 1966.

Thagaard, Tove. "Academic Values and Intellectual Attitudes: Sex Differentiation or Similarity?" *Acta Sociologica* 18 (1975): 36–48.

Tien, H. Yuan. "Mobility, Non-Familial Activity and Fertility." *Demography* 4 (1967): 218–28.

Tobin, Patricia Lysbeth. "Conjugal Role Definitions, Value of Children and Contraceptive Practice." *The Sociological Quarterly* 17 (1976): 314–322.

Toch, Hans. *The Social Psychology of Social Movements.* Indianapolis: Bobbs-Merrill Company, 1965.

Turner, Barbara F., and Joanne Hammer McCaffrey. "Socialization and Career Orientation Among Black and White College Women." *Journal of Vocational Behavior* 5 (1974): 307–319.

Turner, Barbara F., and Castellano B. Turner. "Race, Sex, and Perception of the Occupational Opportunity Structure among College Students." *The Sociological Quarterly* 16 (1975): 345–360.

Turner, Jonathan H. *The Structure of Sociological Theory.* Homewood, Illinois: The Dorsey Press, 1974.

Veevers, J. E. "The Moral Careers of Voluntarily Childless Wives: Notes on the Defense of a Variant World View." *The Family Coordinator* 24 (1975): 473–487.

Veevers, J. E. "The Violation of Fertility Mores: Voluntary Childlessness as Deviant Behavior." *Deviant Behavior and Societal Reactions.* Edited by C. Boydell et al. Toronto: Holt, Rinehard, and Winston, 1972.

Veevers, J. E. "Voluntarily Childless Wives: An Exploratory Study." *Sociology and Social Research: An International Quarterly* 57 (1973): 356–366.

Vinokur-Kaplan, Diane. "Family Planning Decision-Making: A Comparison and Analysis of Parents' Considerations." *Journal of Comparative Family Studies* 8 (1977): 79–98.

Vogel, S. R., I. K. Broverman, D. M. Broverman, F. E. Clarkson, and P. S. Rosenkrantz. "Maternal Employment and Perception of Sex Roles among College Students." *Developmental Psychology* 3 (1970): 384–391.

Waite, Linda J. "Working Wives: 1940–1960." *American Sociological Review* 41 (1976): 65–80.

Warnecke, Richard B. "Non-Intellectual Factors Related to Attrition from a Collegiate Nursing Program." *Journal of Health and Social Behavior* 14 (1973): 153–167.

Whelan, Elizabeth M. *A Baby? . . . Maybe: A Guide to Making the Most Fateful Decision of Your Life.* The Bobbs-Merrill Company, 1975.

Williams. T. E., J. M. Bennett and D. H. Best. "Awareness and Expression of Sex Stereotypes in Young Children." *Developmental Psycology* 11 (1975): 635–642.

Willis, Robert J. "A New Approach to the Economic Theory of Fertility Behavior." *Journal of Political Economy* 81 (1973): 514–564.

Young, Christabel M. "Work Sequences of Women During the Family Life Cycle." *Journal of Marriage and the Family* 40 (1974): 401–411.

Zanar, Eileen. "Reentry Ripoff: One Housewife's Expose." *Ms. Magazine,* Oct. 1977.

Zellman, Gail L. "The Role of Structural Factors in Limiting Women's Institutional Participation." *Journal of Social Issues* 32 (1976): 33–46.

BACKGROUND VARIABLES

I.D. number _____ School_____

Date_____

Please fill in the following information to the best of your ability.

1. Age_____
2. (Ex-) Husband's Age_____
3. (Ex-) Husband's Occupation_____
4. Last Year of School Completed by (Ex-) Husband_____
5. Total Annual Family Income (If this has changed since a divorce or for other reasons, please note two categories and specify which is your current income.)   _____$ '9,999 and below
    _____ 10,000-14,999.
    _____ 15,000-19,999.
    _____ 20,000-24,999.
    _____ 25,000-29,999.
    _____ 30,000 and over

6. Please list your sources of income (e.g., husband's income, Social Security, etc.)

    _____

    _____

    _____

    _____

7. Father's Occupation_____
8. Last Year of School Completed by Father_____
9. Mother's Occupation_____
10. Last Year of School Completed by Mother_____
11. Number of Brothers and Sisters _____
12. Ages of Brothers and Sisters (please list ages) _____

    _____

13. Religious Affiliation_____

INTERVIEW SCHEDULE

I.D.#_____ School _____

Date_____

First, I would like to ask you some questions about your premarital and marital history including what you did before you were married and during your early marriage particularly with regard to working, having children, going to school and other major activities. If any of these questions seem to be too personal, or you'd rather not answer them for any reason, please let me know and we will move on to other areas of the interview.

1. Are you presently married?

       _____yes (If yes, skip to Item 4.)

       _____no

2. If the answer to the first question is no, are you

       _____separated

       _____divorced

       _____other (specify)

3. How long have you been separated/divorced/other?

    _____

4. How long have you been/were you married? (If there has been more than one marriage, get data for all marriages.)

    _____

5. How old were you when you got married?

    _____

6. How long did you know your husband before you were married?

    _____

7. What did you do during your day before you were married?

8. What did you do during your day during your early marriage?

I.D.# _____

9. Do you remember if there was any particular point when these activities changed? (Specify and elaborate further on divorce, etc.)

10. Had you been to college before you were married?

_____yes

_____no (If no, skip to Item 20.)

11. At what point did you leave college?

_____before marriage

_____upon marrying

_____shortly after marriage

_____when the first child was born

_____never

_____other (specify)

12. What was your college status when you left?

_____freshman

_____sophomore

_____junior

_____senior

_____graduate student

13. What was your major?

_____ _____

14. Do you remember changing majors?

_____yes

_____no (If no, skip to Item 16.)

15. How often did you change majors?

_____once

_____twice

_____three or more times

I.D.# _____

16. Did you complete a degree?

                                  ____yes (If yes, skip to Item 18.)

                                  ____no

17. Briefly explain why you did not/could not complete a degree.

18. Did you intend to pursue a career related to your major field?

                                  ____yes (If yes, skip to Item 20.)

                                  ____no

                                  ____didn't know

19. Did you intend to pursue work at all?

                                  ____yes

                                  ____no

                                  ____didn't know

20. Did you ever go (back) to college later during your marriage?

                                  ____(If yes, answer Items 12–19.)

                                  ____no (If no, skip to Item 27.)

21. What stage would you say your family was in when you went (back) to college?

    ____ just beginning your family

    ____had completed childbearing and had all the children you wished to have

    ____children were beginning to leave home

    ____other (specify)

22. How long were you in college at that time?

23. Why did you return to college at that time?

24. If you had wanted to pursue the field you studied while you were in college, do you think you would have had to move to follow the job market?

                                  ____yes

                                  ____no (If no, skip to Item 26.)

                                  ____don't know

I.D.# _____

25. How do you think it would have affected your marriage if you had had to or wanted to move to follow the job market?

26. Were you in college when you met your husband?

      _____yes (If yes, skip to Item 28.)

      _____no

27. What were you doing when you met your husband?

28. Did you assume that you would take part in your husband's career or help support your husband emotionally while he pursued his career or job?

      _____yes

      _____no

      _____didn't know

29. Did you assume that you would help support your husband financially while he pursued his career or job?

      _____yes

      _____no

      _____didn't know

30. Did you work after marriage?

      _____yes

      _____no (If no, skip to Item 34.)

31. What type of job did you have?

32. How long did you work?

33. Did you see your own work as secondary?

      _____yes

      _____no

I.D.# _____

34. When did you and your husband seriously think about having children?

_____before marriage

_____during the first year of marriage

_____never thought about it

_____other (specify)

35. How many children do you have?

_____

36. How old were you when the first child was born?

_____1st child

_____2nd child

_____3rd child

_____4th child (account for all children)

37. Did you plan the number of children you intended to have?

_____yes

_____no

_____tried to

38. Did you plan the spacing of your children?

_____yes

_____no

_____tried to

39. How many children did you want?

_____

40. How many children would you consider ideal?

_____

41. Why do you consider this number ideal?

I.D.#_____

42. Would you say that luck or fate plays a part in the number of children you have?

               _____yes

               _____no

               _____undecided

43. Can you give a reason for your last answer?

44. Do you approve or disapprove of birth control?

               _____strongly approve

               _____somewhat approve

               _____neither approve nor disapprove

               _____somewhat disapprove

               _____strongly disapprove

45. How many times did you become pregnant that you wished you hadn't?

               _____

46. Have you ever really worried about becoming pregnant?

               _____yes

               _____very worried

               _____somewhat worried

               _____no

               _____never thought about it

47. Would you say that generally speaking you planned for the future or did you take each day as it came during your early marriage and childbearing years?

               _____planned for future

               _____took each day as it came

48. Have you ever relocated/Did you ever relocate to follow your husband during your marriage?

               _____yes

               _____no (If no, skip to Item 50.)

I.D.# _____

49. How did the move restructure your daily activities? Can you tell me what you did during the day after the move?

50. What stage would you say your family is in now?

_____just beginning your family

_____have completed childbearing and have all the children you intend to have

_____children are beginning to leave home

_____children have left home

_____other (specify)

Now I would like to ask you some questions about your entry/reentry into college and some of your plans for the future.

51. How do you plan to spend your time after/now that the children are gone? Briefly explain.

52. Are you thinking about getting a job at this time?

_____yes

_____very much

_____somewhat

_____no (If no, skip to Item 55.)

_____undecided

53. Do you recall at what point you started thinking about working? Please explain.

I.D.#_____

54. Why do you want to go to work at this time?

55. Are you thinking about pursuing a career at this time?

_____yes

_____very much

_____somewhat

_____no (If no, skip to Item 58.)

_____undecided

56. Do you recall at what point you started thinking about a career? Please explain.

57. Why do you want to pursue a career at this time?

58. If you do not plan to pursue a job or career at this time, do you have other goals in mind?

_____yes

_____no (If no, skip to Item 62.)

_____undecided

59. Briefly, what is the nature of your goals?

60. At what point did you decide to pursue these goals?

61. Why did you decide to pursue these goals?

I.D.# _____

62. Do you remember whether your husband made a strong career push at any particular point during your marriage?

                        _____yes

                        _____no (If no, skip to Item 64.)

                        _____don't remember

63. At what stage of the marriage did your husband make his career push?

64. Briefly describe how you feel about going (back) to college.

65. What do you do during your day now that you are in college?

66. What did you do during your day just before you decided to go (back) to college?

At this time I would like to ask you about how other people have reacted to your new position as student.

(Ask next four questions only if the woman is married. If she is not married, skip to Item 71.)

67. How has your husband reacted to these changes in your life? Briefly describe.

I.D.#_____

68. Do you ever argue with your husband?

                  _____yes

                  _____frequently

                  _____occasionally

                  _____rarely

                  _____no (If no, skip to Item 71.)

69. Would you say you argue more or less since you went back to school?

                  _____more

                  _____much more

                  _____a little more

                  _____about the same

                  _____less

                  _____a little less

                  _____much less

70. What do you argue about?

71. Do you still have children living at home?

                  _____yes

                  _____no (If no, skip to Item 75.)

72. How many children are living at home?

73. What are their ages?

74. How have they reacted to these changes in your life? Briefly describe.

I.D.# _____

75. Do you feel it is important for a mother to stay with her children full-time until they are a certain age?

_____yes

_____very important

_____pretty important

_____slightly important

_____no (If no, skip to Item 77.)

_____undecided

76. At what age do you feel children no longer need full-time mothering?

_____

77. How have your friends reacted to these changes in your life? Briefly describe.

78. Do you feel you have more or less friends since you returned to school?

_____more

_____many more

_____a few more

_____about the same number

_____fewer

_____only a few less

_____much fewer

79. What do you attribute this to?

Now, I am going to ask you about school and how your school commitments relate to your family commitments.

80. Are you currently working toward a particular degree?

_____yes

_____no (If no, skip to Item 85.)

_____undecided

I.D.# _____

81. What field are you anticipating receiving your degree in?

   _____

82. Why did you choose that particular field?

83. Are the courses that are required appropriate for where you are headed?

   _____ yes

   _____ very appropriate

   _____ somewhat appropriate

   _____ no

   _____ not particularly appropriate

   _____ not at all appropriate

   _____ undecided

84. What do you attribute this to?

85. Do you think that there is a lot of competition in school?

   _____ yes

   _____ very competitive

   _____ somewhat competitive

   _____ no (If no, skip to Item 87.)

   _____ not too competitive

   _____ not at all competitive

   _____ undecided

86. What do you attribute the competition to?

87. Do your commitments to marriage and/or family interfere with your school work?

   _____ yes

   _____ very much

   _____ somewhat

   _____ occasionally

   _____ no

   _____ undecided

I.D. # _____

88. Do your commitments to school interfere with your marriage and/or family relationships?

_____yes

_____very much

_____somewhat

_____occasionally

_____no

_____undecided

89. Do other people help you with the housework?

_____yes

_____no (If no, skip to Item 91.)

90. Who helps you with the housework?

91. About how many hours a week do you spend on housework?

_____ 0-5

_____ 6-10

_____11-15

_____16-20

_____21-25

_____26-30

_____over 30

92. How does this compare to the time you spent on housework before you went back to college? (Give previous number of hours spent.)

_____

93. How has going back to school changed your attitude toward yourself? Briefly describe.

94. How has going back to school changed your attitude toward your husband? (for married women only)

I.D.#_____

95. How has going back to school changed your attitude toward your children?

96. Do you see your age as an advantage or a disadvantage in terms of reaching your goals?

_____advantage

_____disadvantage

_____neither

_____haven't thought about it

_____other (specify)

97. What do you attribute this to?

98. If you see your age as a disadvantage, how will you work around it?

99. Have you ever been discriminated against or felt discriminated against as a woman seeking employment or other opportunities?

_____yes

_____no (If no, skip to Item 101.)

_____possibly

100. Describe how and when briefly.

I.D.# _____

101. Do you feel that there is a good psychological support structure in the university for entering or reentering women?

           _____yes

           _____no

           _____unaware of such a structure

102. Do you feel like part of the setting or like an outsider in the university/college?

           _____part of setting

           _____outsider

           _____other (specify)

103. Briefly explain why you feel the way you do.

104. Have any professors taken a special interest in you?

           _____yes

           _____no

105. How do you feel you have been doing in college since you returned?

           _____very well

           _____somewhat well

           _____alright

           _____somewhat poorly

           _____very poorly

106. Do you know what your G.P.A. is since you came back to college?

           _____yes

           _____(actual G.P.A.)

           _____no

107. What do you intend to use your education for?

           _____personal growth

           _____new career

           _____getting updated on new material for job

           _____other (specify)

I.D.#_____

108. Do you think that your education will enable you to have an effect on any part of society?

     _____yes

     _____no (If no, skip to Item 110.)

     _____don't know

109. What kind of an effect do you think you could have?

110. Overall, how satisfied do you feel with the way you deal with your current activities in life?

     _____very satisfied

     _____somewhat satisfied

     _____neutral

     _____somewhat dissatisfied

     _____very dissatisfied

111. In general, how happy would you say you are?

     _____very happy

     _____somewhat happy

     _____neutral

     _____somewhat unhappy

     _____very unhappy

112. Why do you feel this way?

113. Do you see pressures stemming from:

     _____time

     _____home

     _____husband

     _____children

     _____school

     _____self

     _____other (specify)

I.D.# _____

114. In general, how do you cope with pressure?

_____by changing others' expectations of you

_____by changing your expectations of yourself

_____by altering your behavior in an attempt to meet all expectations

115. What are your main reasons for returning to the university/college? Please summarize.

116. Why did you choose this particular school?

117. Do you think this interview has covered important aspects of you life? Have any important points been left out? Would you add any thing to the questionnaire?

Index